Christina Georgina Rossetti, William Michael Rossetti

New Poems

Christina Georgina Rossetti, William Michael Rossetti
New Poems
ISBN/EAN: 9783744714006
Printed in Europe, USA, Canada, Australia, Japan
Cover: Foto ©Thomas Meinert / pixelio.de

More available books at **www.hansebooks.com**

NEW POEMS

BY

CHRISTINA ROSSETTI

NEW POEMS

BY

CHRISTINA ROSSETTI

HITHERTO UNPUBLISHED OR
UNCOLLECTED

EDITED BY

WILLIAM MICHAEL ROSSETTI

I rated to the full amount
Must render mine account

New York
MACMILLAN AND CO.
AND LONDON
1896

All rights reserved

Norwood Press
J. S. Cushing & Co. — Berwick & Smith
Norwood Mass. U.S.A.

TO

ALGERNON CHARLES SWINBURNE

GENEROUS EULOGIST OF

CHRISTINA ROSSETTI

WHO HAILED HIS GENIUS AND PRIZED HIMSELF

THE GREATEST OF LIVING BRITISH POETS

MY OLD AND CONSTANT FRIEND

I DEDICATE THIS BOOK

W. M. R.

PREFACE

My sister Christina Georgina Rossetti — beloved by me, admired, and I may say reverenced — died on 29 December 1894, aged 64. There was an immediate, a very wide, and an exceedingly strong outburst of eulogy of her in the public press, both as woman and as poetess; an outburst which must have fully convinced me — had I not known it already — that she is regarded as one of the truly important figures in British poetical literature of the nineteenth century.

It will readily be supposed that I do not contest that opinion; and, as soon as the conditions admitted of it, I resolved to put into print any verses of hers which I could find, such as would sustain her poetical reputation, or be of substantial interest as showing the growth of her mind. I looked carefully through the materials which she had left behind her; found many things which I remembered, and others of which I knew little or nothing; and perceived that the amount of her unpublished verse was considerably in excess of what I had surmised. The result is that I now present to the reader a rather large volume, and not (as I had expected) a small one.

A glance at the Contents will at once exhibit the arrangement which has been adopted in this collection. There are four headings: — 1, General Poems; 2, Devotional Poems; 3, Italian; and 4, Juvenilia.

Nos. 1 and 2 explain themselves well enough. As to No. 3, it may suffice to say that I am well aware these Italian writings will obtain few readers in this country; but Christina was partly an Italian, and it may be that her compatriots of the South will not be wholly unheedful of what she composed in their tongue. I consider that her Italian verses are, from a poetical point of view, every bit as good as her English verses, while the exquisite limpidity of the Italian language adds something to the flow of their music. There are likely to be some inaccuracies and blemishes of diction, but perhaps only a native eye would detect these — mine barely does. Section 4 is, of course, of less intrinsic worth than the other sections, but I am in hopes that it will count as not wholly uninteresting. I class among the Juvenilia all that the authoress wrote before attaining (on 5 December

PREFACE

1847) the full age of seventeen; all these things, and nothing else. In this last-named section I make no distinction of subject-matter, nor yet of language. Everything is ranged in order of date, precise or approximate; the like order (it will be perceived) is observed in the other sections respectively.

A few remarks on the sources of the volume may be desirable.

As soon as Christina began writing verse, 27 April 1842, her compositions were copied into little note-books. These are seventeen in number, going on to 11 June 1866. The date of each piece is accurately recorded. At first the handwriting is that of our elder sister Maria; it is only on 17 November 1847, when she was close on seventeen years of age, that Christina began trusting to her own extremely neat but (for several years) rather timid and formal script. Persons familiar with the dates of her publications will observe that the note-books go up to about the time when she printed the volume named *The Prince's Progress and other Poems*, leaving untouched the date, 1881, of her later volume, *A Pageant and other Poems*. These seventeen note-books are the source of a considerable majority of the items in our present volume; and they would enable me (as already implied) to fix the dates not only of what I am now printing, but also of the contents of my sister's first two published volumes. No little interest, I think, attaches to dates, and, if I have the opportunity at some future time, I shall feel it a satisfaction to show what were the dates of her poems previously known to readers.

Supplementing the note-books, my sources are — the privately-printed volume of 1847, called *Verses;* another privately-printed book, *Hadrian's Address to his Soul; The Germ;* the original *Goblin Market* volume, containing three compositions not afterwards reprinted; Christina's prose book entitled *Commonplace and other Stories,* and (for Italian translations) a copy of her *Singsong;* three volumes of selected hymns and devotional verse, named individually in my notes; Mr. Caine's compilation, *Sonnets of Three Centuries;* some magazines and reviews, such as *Macmillan's Magazine, The Athenæum,* etc.; and various scattered MSS. which remained in her own possession. My notes give any needful particulars as to this matter, and as to some other points which the reader may prefer to see mentioned. It seems more than probable that other verses by my sister, as yet uncollected, were printed here and there in magazines etc., but I have not as yet succeeded in tracing any such. Possibly also—spite of painstaking inspection on my part—some passages included in the present volume from MSS. may have appeared elsewhere, printed under altered headings; I have done my best to avoid any such repetition.

I have reprinted everything by my sister which I find already published, not in volume form. I omit the more unsuccessful items in her early book of *Verses;* and I omit also a certain—not large—number of compositions in MS., whether in the note-books or otherwise, which appear to me to represent her less than well.

It is for the reader to form his own opinion whether the contents of the present volume are good, bad, or indifferent. But he may perhaps expect me to give some intimation as to the value which I attach to them, in comparison with those poems which my sister saw fit to publish during her lifetime. Let me, then, say briefly that I conceive *some* of the compositions herein contained to be up to the level of Christina Rossetti's best work, and the great majority of them to be well up to her average.

But, if such is the case (it may be asked), why did she not publish these verses herself? As to most of the items I see no special reason, unless it be this—that, in point of subject or sentiment, they often resemble, more or less, some of those examples which she *did* print; and she may have thought that the public, while willing to have one such specimen, would be quite contented to lack a second. Christina, I take leave to say, did decidedly discern herself to be a poetess, in the right sense of the word; but her self-estimate was always a modest one, and she had not the least inclination to thrust herself, her emotions, or her verses, upon the attention of any person. Now that she is gone, leaving behind her a literary reputation not a little covetable, it seems reasonable to apply a different rule to the question. If readers like these additional evidences of her powers, if they entertain much the same opinion of them that I do, well and good; if not, let the book be regarded as a superfluity, and let her name as a poetess continue to rest upon what she herself elected to give to the world.

Christina's habits of composing were eminently of the spontaneous kind. I question her having ever once deliberated with herself whether or not she would write something or other, and then, after thinking out a subject, having proceeded to treat it in regular spells of work. Instead of this, something impelled her feelings, or "came into her head," and her hand obeyed the dictation. I suppose she scribbled the lines off rapidly enough, and afterwards took whatever amount of pains she deemed requisite for keeping them right in form and expression — for she was quite conscious that a poem demands to be good in execution, as well as genuine in impulse; but (strange as it seems to say so of a sister who, up to the year 1876, was almost constantly in the same house with me) I cannot remember ever seeing her in the act of composition (I take no count here of the *bouts-rimés* sonnets of 1848). She consulted nobody, and solicited no advice; though it is true that with regard to her published volumes — or at any rate the first two of them — my brother volunteered to point out what seemed well adapted for insertion, and what the reverse, and he found her a very willing recipient of his monitions.

The portrait of my sister given in the present volume is taken from a pencil drawing done by Dante Gabriel, which remained quite unnoticed (and by myself forgotten) until I turned it up among her miscellanies after her death. It is much like her, and is possibly the sweetest version of her face that he or anyone ever produced. I should not be surprised if it were a slight study preliminary to the picture *Ecce Ancilla Domini* (National Gallery). She sat for the head there of the Virgin Mary, which is not however in profile. In such case its date cannot be earlier than the middle or later part of 1849, when Christina was eighteen years of age; the head looks to me even younger than that, rather than older.

Apart from this book, my sister's poems are contained in three volumes, published by Messrs. Macmillan — I have already mentioned them; also in the volume named *Singsong*, now in the hands of the same firm; and in the *Verses* (1893) issued by the Society for Promoting Christian Knowledge. Were it to be my privilege at some future day to bring out her Complete Poetical Works on something of the same plan as the present volume — with due regard to dates, etc. — few things would please me better. Her memory is one of my most sacred treasures, and her works and their repute are proportionately dear to me.

WILLIAM M. ROSSETTI.

LONDON, *August* 1895.

CONTENTS

GENERAL POEMS

	PAGE
THE WHOLE HEAD IS SICK AND THE WHOLE HEART FAINT	3
REPINING	4
LADY MONTREVOR	14
SONNETS WRITTEN TO BOUTS-RIMÉS—	
I. "AMID THE SHADES OF A DESERTED HALL"	15
II. "I SIT AMONG GREEN SHADY VALLEYS OFT"	15
III. "WOULDST THOU GIVE ME A HEAVY JEWELLED CROWN"	16
IV. "I SAID WITHIN MYSELF: I AM A FOOL"	17
V. "I SOUGHT AMONG THE LIVING AND I SEEK"	17
VI. "AH WELLADAY AND WHEREFORE AM I HERE?"	18
VII. "AND IS THIS AUGUST WEATHER? NAY, NOT SO"	18
VIII. "METHINKS THE ILLS OF LIFE I FAIN WOULD SHUN"	19
IX. THE PLAGUE	20
X a. "WOULD THAT I WERE A TURNIP WHITE"	20

CONTENTS

	PAGE
SONNETS TO BOUTS-RIMÉS —	
X *b*. "I FANCY THE GOOD FAIRIES DRESSED IN WHITE"	21
X *c*. VANITY FAIR	22
ON KEATS	22
HAVE PATIENCE	23
TO LALLA READING MY VERSES TOPSY-TURVY	25
THREE NUNS	27
THE END OF THE FIRST PART	36
TWO ENIGMAS —	
I. "NAME ANY GENTLEMAN YOU SPY"	37
II. "ME YOU OFTEN MEET"	38
TWO CHARADES —	
I. "MY FIRST IS NO PROOF OF MY SECOND"	38
II. "HOW MANY AUTHORS ARE MY FIRST"	39
LOOKING FORWARD	40
LIFE HIDDEN	41
QUEEN ROSE	42
HOW ONE CHOSE	43
SEEKING REST	45
TWO THOUGHTS OF DEATH	46
THREE MOMENTS	47
IS AND WAS	50
SONG — "WE BURIED HER AMONG THE FLOWERS"	51
ANNIE	52
A DIRGE	54
SONG — "IT IS NOT FOR HER EVEN BROW"	55
A FAIR WORLD THOUGH A FALLEN	56
BOOKS IN THE RUNNING BROOKS	56
THE SUMMER IS ENDED	59

CONTENTS

	PAGE
AFTER ALL	59
FROM THE ANTIQUE — "THE WIND SHALL LULL US YET"	60
TO WHAT PURPOSE IS THIS WASTE?	61
NEXT OF KIN	66
PORTRAITS	67
WHAT?	68
NEAR THE STYX	69
A PAUSE	70
HOLY INNOCENTS	70
SEASONS — "IN SPRINGTIME WHEN THE LEAVES ARE YOUNG"	71
BURIED	72
A WISH	72
TWO PARTED	73
FOR ROSALINE'S ALBUM	74
AUTUMN	74
SEASONS — "CROCUSES AND SNOWDROPS WITHER"	75
BALLAD	75
A SOUL	77
FROM THE ANTIQUE — "IT'S A WEARY LIFE, IT IS, SHE SAID"	78
RESTIVE	79
LONG LOOKED FOR	81
LISTENING	82
THE LAST LOOK	83
I HAVE A MESSAGE UNTO THEE	84
COBWEBS	88
AN AFTER-THOUGHT	89
TO THE END	91
MAY	94

	PAGE
BY THE WATER	95
A CHILLY NIGHT	96
LET PATIENCE HAVE HER PERFECT WORK	98
IN THE LANE	100
ACME	101
A BED OF FORGET-ME-NOTS	102
LOOK ON THIS PICTURE AND ON THIS	103
GONE BEFORE	108
LIGHT LOVE	109
WINTER	112
A TRIAD	113
IN AN ARTIST'S STUDIO	114
INTROSPECTIVE	115
DAY DREAMS	116
A NIGHTMARE (FRAGMENT)	118
FOR ONE SAKE	119
FROM METASTASIO	120
TO-DAY AND TO-MORROW	120
YET A LITTLE WHILE	122
FATHER AND LOVER	124
WHAT GOOD SHALL MY LIFE DO ME?	125
COUSIN KATE	127
SISTER MAUDE	129
PROMISES LIKE PIE-CRUST	130
BETTER SO	131
OUR WIDOWED QUEEN	133
IN PROGRESS	134
SEASONS — "OH THE CHEERFUL BUDDING-TIME!"	135
JUNE	136
JESS AND JILL	137

CONTENTS

	PAGE
HELEN GREY	138
A DUMB FRIEND	139
TO-MORROW	140
MARGERY	141
LAST NIGHT	144
IF	145
SUNSHINE	147
MEETING	148
UNDER WILLOWS	149
A SKETCH	150
IF I HAD WORDS	151
EN ROUTE	152
HUSBAND AND WIFE	154
WHAT TO DO?	156
IN A CERTAIN PLACE	156
CANNOT SWEETEN	158
OF MY LIFE	160
WHAT COMES?	161
LOVE'S NAME	161
BY WAY OF REMEMBRANCE	162
AN ECHO FROM WILLOW-WOOD	164
GOLDEN HOLLY	165
AN ALPHABET	165
COR MIO	168
WHO SHALL SAY?	168
LIFE	169
MEETING	170
LINES — " WHERE ARE THE SONGS I USED TO SING "	171
HADRIAN'S DEATH-SONG TRANSLATED	171
VALENTINES TO MY MOTHER — 1876 TO 1886	172

	PAGE
My Mouse	178
A Poor Old Dog	179
Parted	179
To-day's Burden	180
Counterblast on Penny Trumpet	181
Michael F. M. Rossetti	181
The Way of the World	183
To my Fior-di-Lisa	183
Sleeping at Last	184

DEVOTIONAL POEMS

I do set My Bow in the Cloud	187
Death is swallowed up in Victory	189
A Christmas Carol — "Thank God, thank God, we do believe"	192
For Advent — "Sweet sweet sound of distant waters, falling"	193
✓ Two Pursuits	195
The Watchers	196
Behold, I Stand at the Door and Knock	198
Advent — "Come, Thou dost say to angels"	199
All Saints	200
Eye hath not Seen	201
St. Elizabeth of Hungary	204
Moonshine	204
I look for the Lord	207
The Heart knoweth its own Bitterness — "Weep yet awhile"	208
Whitsun Eve	210

CONTENTS

	PAGE
THERE REMAINETH THEREFORE A REST FOR THE PEOPLE OF GOD — "COME, BLESSED SLEEP, MOST FULL, MOST PERFECT, COME"	211
A HARVEST	212
THE ELEVENTH HOUR	214
FOR UNDER A CRUCIFIX	216
WHO HAVE A FORM OF GODLINESS	216
THERE REMAINETH THEREFORE A REST — "IN THE GRAVE WILL BE NO SPACE"	217
YE HAVE FORGOTTEN THE EXHORTATION	218
UNFORGOTTEN	221
ZION SAID	222
HYMN AFTER GABRIELE ROSSETTI — TWO VERSIONS	223
HOW LONG?	226
A MARTYR — "IT IS OVER THE HORRIBLE PAIN"	227
NOW THEY DESIRE	228
A CHRISTMAS CAROL (FOR MY GODCHILDREN) — "THE SHEPHERDS HAD AN ANGEL"	230
NOT YOURS BUT YOU	232
THE HEART KNOWETH ITS OWN BITTERNESS — "WHEN ALL THE OVER-WORK OF LIFE"	233
A BURDEN	235
ONLY BELIEVE	239
A SHADOW OF DOROTHEA	240
FOR HENRIETTA POLYDORE	242
ASH WEDNESDAY	242
A CHRISTMAS CAROL — "BEFORE THE PALING OF THE STARS"	244
EASTER EVEN	245
THE OFFERING OF THE NEW LAW	247

xxii   CONTENTS

	PAGE
BY THE WATERS OF BABYLON	248
WITHIN THE VEIL	250
OUT OF THE DEEP	250
FOR A MERCY RECEIVED	251
CONFERENCE BETWEEN CHRIST, THE SAINTS, AND THE SOUL	253
COME UNTO ME	255
IN PATIENCE	255
NONE WITH HIM	256
BIRDS OF PARADISE	257
I KNOW YOU NOT	258
THOU ART THE SAME AND THY YEARS SHALL NOT FAIL	260
A CHRISTMAS CAROL — "WHOSO HEARS A CHIMING FOR CHRISTMAS AT THE NIGHEST"	261
CARDINAL NEWMAN	261
YEA, I HAVE A GOODLY HERITAGE	262
A DEATH OF A FIRST-BORN	263
FAINT YET PURSUING	264
HEAVEN OVERARCHES	265

ITALIAN POEMS

VERSI — "FIGLIA, LA MADRE DISSE"	269
L' INCOGNITA	270
NIGELLA	270
CHIESA E SIGNORE	271
IL ROSSEGGIAR DELL' ORIENTE — CANZONIERE — IL CANZONI	272
L' UOMMIBATTO	287

CONTENTS

	PAGE
COR MIO	287
ADRIANO	288
NINNA-NANNA — 33 TRADUZIONI DAL SINGSONG	288
SOGNANDO	302

JUVENILIA

TO MY MOTHER ON THE ANNIVERSARY OF HER BIRTH	305
HYMN	305
LOVE AND HOPE	306
ON ALBINA	306
FORGET ME NOT	307
CHARITY	307
EARTH AND HEAVEN	308
LOVE EPHEMERAL	309
BURIAL ANTHEM	310
SUMMER	311
SERENADE	314
THE END OF TIME	315
AMORE E DOVERE	317
MOTHER AND CHILD	318
ON THE DEATH OF A CAT	319
LOVE ATTACKED	320
LOVE DEFENDED	322
THE MARTYR — "SEE, THE SUN HATH RISEN"	323
THE DYING MAN TO HIS BETROTHED	325
LISETTA ALL' AMANTE	328
THE DEAD BRIDE	329
WILL THESE HANDS NE'ER BE CLEAN?	331
PRESENT AND FUTURE	333

	PAGE
THE TIME OF WAITING	334
TASSO AND LEONORA	337
THE SOLITARY ROSE	337
THE SONG OF THE STAR	338
RESURRECTION EVE	341
THE DEAD CITY	342
THE ROSE	353
I HAVE FOUGHT A GOOD FIGHT	354
WISHES	355
THE DREAM	356
ELEANOR	358
ISIDORA	359
ZARA	362
THE NOVICE	364
IMMALEE	366
LADY ISABELLA	366
NIGHT AND DEATH	367
THE LOTUS-EATERS	370
SONNET FROM THE PSALMS	371
SONG — "THE STREAM MOANETH AS IT FLOWETH"	372
THE WORLD'S HARMONIES	373
THE LAST ANSWER (WRITTEN TO BOUTS-RIMÉS)	375
NOTES BY W. M. ROSSETTI	377

GENERAL POEMS

THE WHOLE HEAD IS SICK AND THE WHOLE HEART FAINT

WOE for the young who say that life is long,
    Who turn from the sun-rising to the West,
    Who feel no pleasure and can find no rest,
Who in the morning sigh for evensong.
Their hearts, weary because of this world's wrong,
    Yearn with a thousand longings unexprest;
    They have a wound no mortal ever drest,
An ill than all earth's remedies more strong.
For them the fount of gladness hath run dry,
    And in all Nature is no pleasant thing;
For them there is no glory in the sky,
    No sweetness in the breezes' murmuring:
They say, "The peace of heaven is placed too high,
    And this earth changeth and is perishing."

6 *December* 1847.

REPINING

SHE sat alway through the long day
Spinning the weary thread away;
And ever said in undertone,
"Come, that I be no more alone."

From early dawn to set of sun
Working, her task was still undone;
And the long thread seemed to increase
Even while she spun and did not cease.
She heard the gentle turtle-dove
Tell to its mate a tale of love;
She saw the glancing swallows fly,
Ever a social company;
She knew each bird upon its nest
Had cheering songs to bring it rest;
None lived alone save only she : —
The wheel went round more wearily;
She wept and said in undertone,
"Come, that I be no more alone."

Day followed day, and still she sighed
For love, and was not satisfied;

REPINING

Until one night, when the moonlight
Turned all the trees to silver-white,
She heard, what ne'er she heard before,
A steady hand undo the door.
The nightingale since set of sun
Her throbbing music had not done,
And she had listened silently;
But now the wind had changed, and she
Heard the sweet song no more, but heard
Beside her bed a whispered word:
"Damsel, rise up; be not afraid;
For I am come at last," it said.

She trembled, though the voice was mild;
She trembled like a frightened child; —
Till she looked up, and then she saw
The unknown speaker without awe.
He seemed a fair young man, his eyes
Beaming with serious charities;
His cheek was white but hardly pale;
And a dim glory like a veil
Hovered about his head, and shone
Through the whole room till night was gone.

So her fear fled; and then she said,
Leaning upon her quiet bed:
"Now thou art come, I prythee stay,
That I may see thee in the day,
And learn to know thy voice, and hear
It evermore calling me near."

He answered, "Rise and follow me."
But she looked upwards wonderingly:
"And whither wouldst thou go, friend? stay
Until the dawning of the day."
But he said: "The wind ceaseth, Maid;
Of chill nor damp be thou afraid."

She bound her hair up from the floor,
And passed in silence from the door.

So they went forth together, he
Helping her forward tenderly.
The hedges bowed beneath his hand;
Forth from the streams came the dry land
As they passed over; evermore
The pallid moonbeams shone before;
And the wind hushed, and nothing stirred;
Not even a solitary bird,
Scared by their footsteps, fluttered by
Where aspen-trees stood steadily.

As they went on, at length a sound
Came trembling on the air around;
The undistinguishable hum
Of life, voices that go and come
Of busy men, and the child's sweet
High laugh, and noise of trampling feet.

Then he said, "Wilt thou go and see?"
And she made answer joyfully:

"The noise of life, of human life,
Of dear communion without strife,
Of converse held 'twixt friend and friend;
Is it not here our path shall end?"
He led her on a little way
Until they reached a hillock: "Stay."

It was a village in a plain.
High mountains screened it from the rain
And stormy wind; and nigh at hand
A bubbling streamlet flowed o'er sand
Pebbly and fine, and sent life up
Green succous stalk and flower-cup.

Gradually, day's harbinger,
A chilly wind began to stir.
It seemed a gentle powerless breeze
That scarcely rustled through the trees;
And yet it touched the mountain's head
And the paths man might never tread.
But hearken: in the quiet weather
Do all the streams flow down together?—
No, 'tis a sound more terrible
Than though a thousand rivers fell.
The everlasting ice and snow
Were loosened then, but not to flow;—
With a loud crash like solid thunder
The avalanche came, burying under
The village; turning life and breath
And rest and joy and plans to death.

"Oh let us fly, for pity fly !
Let us go hence, friend, thou and I.
There must be many regions yet
Where these things make not desolate."

He looked upon her seriously ;
Then said : "Arise and follow me."
The path that lay before them was
Nigh covered over with long grass ;
And many slimy things and slow
Trailed on between the roots below.
The moon looked dimmer than before ;
And shadowy cloudlets floating o'er
Its face sometimes quite hid its light,
And filled the skies with deeper night.

At last, as they went on, the noise
Was heard of the sea's mighty voice ;
And soon the ocean could be seen
In its long restlessness serene.
Upon its breast a vessel rode
That drowsily appeared to nod
As the great billows rose and fell,
And swelled to sink, and sank to swell.

Meanwhile the strong wind had come forth
From the chill regions of the North,
The mighty wind invisible.
And the low waves began to swell ;
And the sky darkened overhead ;
And the moon once looked forth, then fled

Behind dark clouds; while here and there
The lightning shone out in the air,
And the approaching thunder rolled
With angry pealings manifold.
How many vows were made, and prayers
That in safe times were cold and scarce!
Still all availed not; and at length
The waves arose in all their strength,
And fought against the ship, and filled
The ship. Then were the clouds unsealed,
And the rain hurried forth, and beat
On every side and over it.

Some clung together, and some kept
A long stern silence, and some wept.
Many half-crazed looked on in wonder
As the strong timbers rent asunder;
Friends forgot friends, foes fled to foes; —
And still the water rose and rose.

"Ah woe is me! Whom I have seen
Are now as though they had not been.
In the earth there is room for birth,
And there are graves enough in earth;
Why should the cold sea, tempest-torn,
Bury those whom it hath not borne?"

He answered not, and they went on.
The glory of the heavens was gone;
The moon gleamed not nor any star;

Cold winds were rustling near and far,
And from the trees the dry leaves fell
With a sad sound unspeakable.
The air was cold ; till from the South
A gust blew hot, like sudden drouth,
Into their faces ; and a light,
Glowing and red, shone through the night.

A mighty city full of flame
And death and sounds without a name.
Amid the black and blinding smoke,
The people, as one man, awoke.
Oh happy they who yesterday
On the long journey went away !
Whose pallid lips, smiling and chill,
While the flames scorch them smile on still ;
Who murmur not, who tremble not
When the bier crackles fiery hot ;
Who dying said in love's increase,
" Lord, let thy servant part in peace."

Those in the town could see and hear
A shaded river flowing near ;
The broad deep bed could hardly hold
Its plenteous waters calm and cold.
Was flame-wrapt all the city wall,
The city gates were flame-wrapt all.

What was man's strength, what puissance then ?
Women were mighty as strong men.

Some knelt in prayer, believing still,
Resigned unto a righteous will,
Bowing beneath the chastening rod,
Lost to the world, but found of God.
Some prayed for friend, for child, for wife;
Some prayed for faith; some prayed for life;
While some, proud even in death, hope gone,
Steadfast and still, stood looking on.

"Death — death — oh let us fly from death!
Where'er we go it followeth;
All these are dead; and we alone
Remain to weep for what is gone.
What is this thing? thus hurriedly
To pass into eternity;
To leave the earth so full of mirth;
To lose the profit of our birth;
To die and be no more; to cease,
Having numbness that is not peace.
Let us go hence; and, even if thus
Death everywhere must go with us,
Let us not see the change, but see
Those who have been or still shall be."

He sighed, and they went on together.
Beneath their feet did the grass wither;
Across the heaven high overhead
Dark misty clouds floated and fled;
And in their bosom was the thunder,
And angry lightnings flashed out under,

Forked and red and menacing;
Far off the wind was muttering;
It seemed to tell, not understood,
Strange secrets to the listening wood.

Upon its wings it bore the scent
Of blood of a great armament:
Then saw they how on either side
Fields were down-trodden far and wide.
That morning at the break of day
Two nations had gone forth to slay.

As a man soweth so he reaps.
The field was full of bleeding heaps;
Ghastly corpses of men and horses
That met death at a thousand sources;
Cold limbs and putrifying flesh;
Long love-locks clotted to a mesh
That stifled; stiffened mouths beneath
Staring eyes that had looked on death.

But these were dead: these felt no more
The anguish of the wounds they bore
Behold, they shall not sigh again,
Nor justly fear, nor hope in vain.
What if none wept above them? — is
The sleeper less at rest for this?
Is not the young child's slumber sweet
When no man watcheth over it?

These had deep calm; but all around
There was a deadly smothered sound,
The choking cry of agony
From wounded men who could not die;
Who watched the black wing of the raven
Rise like a cloud 'twixt them and heaven,
And in the distance flying fast
Beheld the eagle come at last.

She knelt down in her agony.
"O Lord, it is enough," said she:
"My heart's prayer putteth me to shame;
Let me return to whence I came.
Thou who for love's sake didst reprove,
Forgive me for the sake of love."

December 1847.

LADY MONTREVOR

I DO not look for love that is a dream—
  I only seek for courage to be still;
  To bear my grief with an unbending will,
And when I am a-weary not to seem.
Let the round world roll on; let the sun beam;
  Let the wind blow, and let the rivers fill
  The everlasting sea, and on the hill
The palms almost touch heaven, as children deem.
And, though young spring and summer pass away,
  And autumn and cold winter come again,
  And though my soul, being tired of its pain,
Pass from the ancient earth, and though my clay
  Return to dust, my tongue shall not complain;—
No man shall mock me after this my day.

18 *February* 1848.

SONNETS

Written to Bouts-Rimés

I

AMID the shades of a deserted hall
I stand and think on much that hath been lost.
How long it is since other step has crost
This time-worn floor ! This tapestry is all
Worm-eaten; and these columns rise up tall
    Yet crumbling to decay; where banners tost
    Thin spider's webs hang now; the bitter frost
Has even killed the flowers upon the wall.
Yet once this was a home brimful of life,
    Full of the hopes and fears and love of youth,
        Full of love's language speaking without sound:
Here honour was enshrined and kindly truth;
Hither the young lord brought his blushing wife,
    And here the bridal garlands were unbound.

II

I SIT among green shady valleys oft,
    Listening to echo-winds sighing of woe;
    The grass and flowers are strong and sweet below;
Yea I am tired, and the smooth turf is soft.
I sit and think, and never look aloft,

Save to the tops of a tall poplar-row
That glisten in the wind, whispering low
Of sudden sorrow reaching those who laught.
A very drowsy fountain bubbles near,
    Catching pale sunbeams o'er it wandering;
    Its waters are so clear the stones look through:
Then, sitting by its lazy stream, I hear
    Silence more loud than any other thing,
    What time the trees weep o'er me honey-dew.

III

WOULDST thou give me a heavy jewelled crown
    And purple mantle and embroidered vest?
Dear Child, the colours of the glorious West
Are far more gorgeous when the sun sinks down.
The diadem would only make me frown
    With its own weight; nay give me for my crest
    Pale violets dreaming in perfect rest,
Or rather leaves withered to autumn brown.
A purple flowing mantle would but hinder
    My careless walk, and an embroidered robe
        Would shame me. What is the best man who stept
        On earth more than the naked worm that crept
Over its surface? Earth shall be a cinder;
    Where shall be then the beauty of the globe?

IV

I SAID within myself: "I am a fool
To sigh ever for that which being gone
Cannot return: the sun shines as it shone;
Rejoice."—But who can be made glad by rule?
My heart and soul and spirit are no tool
To play with and direct; my cheek is wan
With memory; and ever and anon
I weep, feeling life is a weary school.
There is much noise and bustle in the street;
It used to be so, and it is so now;
All are the same, and will be many a year.
Spirit that canst not break and wilt not bow,
Fear not the cold, thou who hast born the heat;—
Die if thou wilt, but what hast thou to fear?

V

I SOUGHT among the living, and I seek
Among the dead, for some to love; but few
I found at last, and those had quite run through
Their store of love; and friendship is too weak,
Too cold for me; yet will I never speak,
Telling my heart-want to smooth listeners who
Would wonder smiling; I can bear and do—
Hot shame shall dry no tears upon my cheek.
So, when my dust shall mix with other dust,

When I shall have found quiet in decay,
  And lie at ease and cease like a mere thought,—
  Those whom I loved, thinking on me, shall not
Grieve with a measure, saying, "Now we must
  Weep for a little ere we laugh to-day."

VI

AH welladay and wherefore am I here?
  I sit alone all day, I sit and think—
I watch the sun arise, I watch it sink,
And feel no soul-light, though the day is clear.
Surely it is a folly, it is mere
  Madness, to stand for ever on the brink
  Of dark despair, and yet not break the link
That makes me scorned who cannot be held dear.
I will have done with it; I will not stand
  And fear on without hope, and tremble thus,
    Look for the break of day and miss it ever.
  Although my heart be broken, they shall never
  Say, "She was glad to sojourn among us,
Thankful if one would take her by the hand."

VII

AND is this August weather? Nay, not so.
  With the long rain the cornfield waxeth dark.
  How the cold rain comes pouring down! and hark
To the chill wind whose measured pace and slow
Seems still to linger, being loth to go.

I cannot stand beside the sea and mark
Its grandeur — it's too wet for that: no lark
In this drear season cares to sing or show.
And, since its name is August, all men find
   Fire not allowable; winter foregone
      Had more of sunlight and of glad warmth more.
   I shall be fain to run upon the shore
      And mark the rain.   Hath the sun ever shone?
Cheer up! there can be nothing worse to mind.

VIII

METHINKS the ills of life I fain would shun;
   But then I must shun life, which is a blank.
Even in my childhood oft my spirit sank,
Thinking of all that had still to be done.
Among my many friends there is not one
   Like her with whom I sat upon the bank
   Willow-o'ershadowed, from whose lips I drank
A love more pure than streams that sing and run.
But many times that joy has cost a sigh;
   And many times I in my heart have sought
      For the old comfort and not found it yet.
Surely in that calm day when I shall die
   The painful thought will be a blessed thought,
      And I shall sorrow that I must forget.

IX—THE PLAGUE

"LISTEN, the last stroke of death's noon has
    struck—.
The plague is come," a gnashing Madman said,
And laid him down straightway upon his bed.
His writhèd hands did at the linen pluck;
Then all is over. With a careless chuck
    Among his fellows he is cast. How sped
    His spirit matters little : many dead
Make men hard-hearted.— "Place him on the truck.
Go forth into the burial-ground and find
    Room at so much a pitful for so many.
    One thing is to be done ; one thing is clear :
Keep thou back from the hot unwholesome wind,
    That it infect not thee." Say, is there any
    Who mourneth for the multitude dead here?

August 1848.

X *a*

WOULD that I were a turnip white,
        Or raven black,
        Or miserable hack
Dragging a cab from left to right ;
Or would I were the showman of a sight,
Or weary donkey with a laden back,
        Or racer in a sack,
Or freezing traveller on an Alpine height ;

Or would I were straw-catching as I drown
(A wretched landsman I who cannot swim),
   Or watching a lone vessel sink,
Rather than writing : I would change my pink
Gauze for a hideous yellow satin gown
With deep-cut scolloped edges and a rim.

X *b*

I FANCY the good fairies dressed in white,
   Glancing like moonbeams through the shadows
      black ;
Without much work to do for king or hack.
Training perhaps some twisted branch aright ;
Or sweeping faded autumn-leaves from sight
   To foster embryo life ; or binding back
   Stray tendrils ; or in ample bean-pod sack
Bringing wild honey from the rocky height ;
Or fishing for a fly lest it should drown ;
   Or teaching water-lily heads to swim,
      Fearful that sudden rain might make them sink ;
      Or dyeing the pale rose a warmer pink ;
Or wrapping lilies in their leafy gown,
   Yet letting the white peep beyond the rim.

↘ x c—VANITY FAIR

SOME ladies dress in muslin full and white,
  Some gentlemen in cloth succinct and black; ·
Some patronize a dog-cart, some a hack,
Some think a painted clarence only right.
Youth is not always such a pleasing sight,
  Witness a man with tassels on his back;
  Or woman in a great-coat like a sack
Towering above her sex with horrid height.
If all the world were water fit to drown,
  There are some whom you would not teach to swim,
    Rather enjoying if you saw them sink;
    Certain old ladies dressed in girlish pink,
With roses and geraniums on their gown:—
  Go to the Bason, poke them o'er the rim.

Circa 1848.

ON KEATS

A GARDEN in a garden: a green spot
  Where all is green: most fitting slumber-place
  For the strong man grown weary of a race
Soon over. Unto him a goodly lot
Hath fallen in fertile ground; there thorns are not,
  But his own daisies; silence, full of grace,
  Surely hath shed a quiet on his face;
His earth is but sweet leaves that fall and rot.

What was his record of himself, ere he
   Went from us? "Here lies one whose name was
      writ
   In water." While the chilly shadows flit
   Of sweet St. Agnes' Eve, while basil springs —
   His name, in every humble heart that sings,
Shall be a fountain of love, verily.

   18 *January* 1849 (Eve of St. Agnes).

HAVE PATIENCE

THE goblets all are broken,
   The pleasant wine is spilt,
   The songs cease. If thou wilt,
Listen, and hear truth spoken.
We take thought for the morrow,
   And know not we shall see it;
We look on death with sorrow,
   And cannot flee it.
Youth passes like the lightning,
   Not to return again, —
Just for a little bright'ning
   The confines of a plain,
Gilding the spires, and whitening
   The gravestones and the slain.
Youth passes like the odour
   From the white rose's cup
   When the hot sun drinks up

The dew that overflowed her:
Then life forsakes the petals
  That had been very fair;
  No beauty lingers there,
    And no bee settles.
But, when the rose is dead
    And the leaves fallen,
And when the earth has spread
    A snow-white pall on,
The thorn remains, once hidden
    By the green growth above it —
A darksome guest unbidden,
    With none to love it.
Manhood is turbulent,
    And old age tires;
That hath no still content,
    This no desires.
The present hath even less
    Joy than the past,
      And more cares fret it: —
Life is a weariness
    From first to last; —
      Let us forget it.
Fill high and deep! — But how?
  The goblets all are broken.
Nay then, have patience now:
  For this is but a token
We soon shall have no need
    Of such to cheer us;
The palm-branches decreed

And crowns to be our meed
Are very near us.
23 *January* 1849.

TO LALLA

READING MY VERSES TOPSY-TURVY

DARLING little Cousin,
With your thoughtful look
Reading topsy-turvy
From a printed book

English hieroglyphics,
More mysterious
To you than Egyptian
Ones would be to us ; —

Leave off for a minute
Studying, and say
What is the impression
That those marks convey.

Only solemn silence
And a wondering smile :
But your eyes are lifted
Unto mine the while.

In their gaze so steady
  I can surely trace
That a happy spirit
  Lighteth up your face ;

Tender happy spirit,
  Innocent and pure,
Teaching more than science,
  And than learning more.

How should I give answer
  To that asking look?
Darling little Cousin,
  Go back to your book.

Read on : if you knew it,
  You have cause to boast :
You are much the wiser
  Though I know the most.

24 *January* 1849.

THREE NUNS

I

*Sospira questo core
E non so dir perchè.*

SHADOW, shadow on the wall,
   Spread thy shelter over me;
Wrap me with a heavy pall,
   With the dark that none may see:
Fold thyself around me, come;
Shut out all the troublesome
Noise of life; I would be dumb.

Shadow, thou hast reached my feet;
   Rise and cover up my head;
Be my stainless winding-sheet,
   Buried before I am dead.
Lay thy cool upon my breast:
Once I thought that joy was best,
Now I only care for rest.

By the grating of my cell
   Sings a solitary bird;
Sweeter than the vesper bell,
   Sweetest song was ever heard.[1]

---

[1] "Sweetest eyes were ever seen." — E. B. BROWNING.

Sing upon thy living tree;
Happy echoes answer thee;
Happy songster, sing to me.

When my yellow hair was curled,
   Though men saw and called me fair,
I was weary in the world,
   Full of vanity and care.
Gold was left behind, curls shorn,
When I came here; that same morn
Made a bride no gems adorn.

Here wrapt in my spotless veil,
   Curtained from intruding eyes,
I whom prayers and fasts turn pale
   Wait the flush of Paradise.
But the vigil is so long
My heart sickens: — sing thy song,
Blythe bird that canst do no wrong.

Sing on, making me forget
   Present sorrow and past sin.
Sing a little longer yet:
   Soon the matins will begin;
And I must turn back again
To that aching, worse than pain, —
I must bear and not complain.

Sing; that in thy song I may
    Dream myself once more a child
In the green woods far away,
    Plucking clematis and wild
Hyacinth, till pleasure grew
Tired, yet so was pleasure too,
Resting with no work to do.

In the thickest of the wood
    I remember long ago
How a stately oaktree stood
    With a sluggish pool below
Almost shadowed out of sight;
On the waters dark as night
Water-lilies lay like light.

There, while yet a child, I thought
    I could live as in a dream;
Secret, neither found nor sought;
    Till the lilies on the stream,
Pure as virgin purity,
Would seem scarce too pure for me:—
Ah but that can never be!

II

*Sospirerà d'amore,
Ma non lo dice a me.*

I loved him; yes, where was the sin?
　I loved him with my heart and soul;
　But I pressed forward to no goal,
There was no prize I strove to win.
Show me my sin that I may see:
Throw the first stone, thou Pharisee.

I loved him, but I never sought
　That he should know that I was fair.
　I prayed for him; was my sin prayer?
I sacrificed, he never bought;
He nothing gave, he nothing took;
We never bartered look for look.

My voice rose in the sacred choir,
　The choir of nuns: do you condemn
　Even if when kneeling among them
Faith, zeal, and love, kindled a fire,
And I prayed for his happiness
Who knew not; was my error this?

I only prayed that in the end
　His trust and hope may not be vain;
　I prayed not we may meet again:

I would not let our names ascend,
No not to Heaven, in the same breath;
Nor will I join the two in death.

Oh sweet is death, for I am weak
  And weary, and it giveth rest.
  The crucifix lies on my breast,
And all night long it seems to speak
Of rest; I hear it through my sleep,
And the great comfort makes me weep.

Oh sweet is death that bindeth up
  The broken and the bleeding heart.
  The draught chilled, but a cordial part
Lurked at the bottom of the cup;
And for my patience will my Lord
Give an exceeding great reward.

Yea the reward is almost won,
  A crown of glory and a palm.
  Soon I shall sing the unknown psalm;
Soon gaze on light, not on the sun;
And soon with surer faith shall pray
For him, and cease not night nor day.

My life is breaking like a cloud —
  God judgeth not as man doth judge —
  Nay, bear with me: you need not grudge
This peace; the vows that I have vowed

Have all been kept: Eternal Strength
Holds me, though mine own fails at length.

Bury me in the Convent-ground
  Among the flowers that are so sweet;
  And lay a green turf at my feet,
Where thick trees cast a gloom around;
At my head let a cross be, white
Through the long blackness of the night.

Now kneel and pray beside my bed
  That I may sleep being free from pain;
  And pray that I may wake again
After His likeness who hath said
(Faithful is He who promiseth)
We shall be satisfied therewith.

III

> Rispondimi, cor mio,
> Perchè sospiri tu?
> Risponde: Voglio Dio,
> Sospiro per Gesù.

My heart is as a freeborn bird
  Caged in my cruel breast,
That flutters, flutters evermore,
  Nor sings nor is at rest,
But beats against the prison bars,
  As knowing its own nest
Far off beyond the clouded west.

My soul is as a hidden fount
   Shut in by clammy clay,
That struggles with an upward moan,
   Striving to force its way
Up through the turf, over the grass,
   Up up into the day
Where twilight no more turneth grey

Oh for the grapes of the True Vine
   Growing in Paradise,
Whose tendrils join the Tree of Life
   To that which maketh wise —
Growing beside the Living Well
   Whose sweetest waters rise
Where tears are wiped from tearful eyes!

Oh for the waters of that Well
   Round which the Angels stand —
Oh for the Shadow of the Rock
   On my heart's weary land —
Oh for the Voice to guide me when
   I turn to either hand,
Guiding me till I reach Heaven's strand!

Thou world from which I am come out,
   Keep all thy gems and gold;
Keep thy delights and precious things,
   Thou that art waxing old.
My heart shall beat with a new life
   When thine is dead and cold;
When thou dost fear I shall be bold.

When Earth shall pass away with all
  Her pride and pomp of sin,
The City builded without hands
  Shall safely shut me in.
All the rest is but vanity
  Which others strive to win:
Where their hopes end my joys begin.

I will not look upon a rose
  Though it is fair to see:
The flowers planted in Paradise
  Are budding now for me:
Red roses like love visible
  Are blowing on their tree,
Or white like virgin purity.

I will not look unto the sun
  Which setteth night by night:
In the untrodden courts of heaven
  My crown shall be more bright.
Lo in the New Jerusalem
  Founded and built aright
My very feet shall tread on light.

With foolish riches of this world
  I have bought treasure where
Nought perisheth: for this white veil
  I gave my golden hair;
I gave the beauty of my face
  For vigils, fasts, and prayer;
I gave all for this cross I bear.

My heart trembled when first I took
  The vows which must be kept.
At first it was a weariness
  To watch when once I slept:
The path was rough and sharp with thorns;
  My feet bled as I stept;
The cross was heavy and I wept.

While still the names rang in mine ears
  Of daughter, sister, wife,
The outside world still looked so fair
  To my weak eyes, and rife
With beauty, my heart almost failed;
  Then in the desperate strife
I prayed, as one who prays for life,·

Until I grew to love what once
  Had been so burdensome.
So now, when I am faint because
  Hope deferred seems to numb
My heart, I yet can plead, and say,
  Although my lips are dumb—
The Spirit and the Bride say, Come.

12 *February* 1849 to 10 *May* 1850.

THE END OF THE FIRST PART

MY happy happy dream is finished with,
  My dream in which alone I lived so long.
My heart slept — woe is me, it wakeneth ;
  Was weak — I thought it strong.

Oh weary wakening from a life-true dream !
  Oh pleasant dream from which I wake in pain !
I rested all my trust on things that seem,
  And all my trust is vain.

I must pull down my palace that I built,
  Dig up the pleasure-gardens of my soul ;
Must change my laughter to sad tears for guilt,
  My freedom to control.

Now all the cherished secrets of my heart,
  Now all my hidden hopes, are turned to sin.
Part of my life is dead, part sick, and part
  Is all on fire within.

The fruitless thought of what I might have been,
  Haunting me ever, will not let me rest.
A cold North wind has withered all my green,
  My sun is in the West.

But, where my palace stood, with the same stone
　I will uprear a shady hermitage :
And there my spirit shall keep house alone,
　　Accomplishing its age.

There other garden-beds shall lie around,
　Full of sweet-briar and incense-bearing thyme :
There I will sit, and listen for the sound
　　Of the last lingering chime.

18 *April* 1849.

TWO ENIGMAS

I

NAME any gentleman you spy,
　And there's a chance that he is I.
Go out to angle, and you may
Catch me on a propitious day.
Booted and spurred, their journey ended,
The weary are by me befriended.
If roasted meat should be your wish,
I am more needful than a dish.
I am acknowledgedly poor ;
Yet my resources are no fewer
Than all the trades — there is not one
But I profess, beneath the sun.

I bear a part in many a game ;
My worth may change, I am the same :
Sometimes, by you expelled, I roam
Forth from the sanctuary of home.

II

Me you often meet
In London's crowded street,
And merry children's voices my resting-place proclaim.
Pictures and prose and verse
Compose me — I rehearse
Evil and good and folly, and call each by its name.
I make men glad, and I
Can bid their senses fly,
And festive echoes know me of Isis and of Cam.
But give me to a friend,
And amity will end,
Though he may have the temper and meekness of a lamb.

Spring 1849.

TWO CHARADES

I

MY first is no proof of my second,
    Though my second's a proof of my first.
If I were my whole, I should tell you
    Quite freely my best and my worst.

One clue more : — If you fail to discover
   My meaning, you're blind as a mole;
But, if you will frankly confess it,
   You show yourself clearly my whole.

II

How many authors are my first!
   And I shall be so too
Unless I finish speedily
   That which I have to do.

My second is a lofty tree
   And a delicious fruit;
This in the hot-house flourishes —
   That amid rocks takes root.

My whole is an immortal queen
   Renowned in classic lore:
Her a god won without her will,
   And her a goddess bore.

Spring 1849.

LOOKING FORWARD

SLEEP, let me sleep, for I am sick of care;
   Sleep, let me sleep, for my pain wearies me.
Shut out the light; thicken the heavy air
With drowsy incense; let a distant stream
Of music lull me, languid as a dream,
   Soft as the whisper of a summer sea.

Pluck me no rose that groweth on a thorn,
   Nor myrtle white and cold as snow in June,
Fit for a virgin on her marriage morn:
But bring me poppies brimmed with sleepy death,
And ivy choking what it garlandeth,
   And primroses that open to the moon.

Listen, the music swells into a song,
   A simple song I loved in days of yore;
The echoes take it up and up along
The hills, and the wind blows it back again. —
Peace, peace, there is a memory in that strain
   Of happy days that shall return no more.

Oh peace! your music wakeneth old thought,
   But not old hope that made my life so sweet,
Only the longing that must end in nought.
Have patience with me, friends, a little while:
For soon, where you shall dance and sing and smile,
   My quickened dust may blossom at your feet.

Sweet thought that I may yet live and grow green,
    That leaves may yet spring from the withered root,
And birds and flowers and berries half unseen;
Then, if you haply muse upon the past,
Say this: Poor child, she has her wish at last;
    Barren through life, but in death bearing fruit.

8 *June* 1849.

LIFE HIDDEN

ROSES and lilies grow above the place
    Where she sleeps the long sleep that doth not dream.
If we could look upon her hidden face,
    Nor shadow would be there, nor garish gleam
    Of light; her life is lapsing like a stream
That makes no noise but floweth on apace
    Seawards, while many a shade and shady beam
Vary the ripples in their gliding chase.
She doth not see, but knows; she doth not feel,
    And yet is sensible; she hears no sound,
        Yet counts the flight of time and doth not err.
        Peace far and near, peace to ourselves and her:
    Her body is at peace in holy ground,
Her spirit is at peace where Angels kneel.

23 *July* 1849.

QUEEN ROSE

THE jessamine shows like a star;
  The lilies sway like sceptres slim;
Fair clematis from near and far
  Sets from forth its wayward tangled whim;
  Curved meadowsweet blooms rich and dim;—
But yet a rose is fairer far.

The jessamine is odorous; so
  Maid-lilies are, and clematis;
And where tall meadowsweet-flowers grow
  A rare and subtle perfume is;—
  What can there be more choice than these?—
A rose when it doth bud and blow.

Let others choose sweet jessamine,
  Or weave their lily-crown aright,
And let who love it pluck and twine
  Loose clematis, or draw delight
  From meadowsweets' cluster downy white—
The rose, the perfect rose, be mine.

16 *August* 1849.

HOW ONE CHOSE

"BEYOND the sea, in a green land
    Where only rivers are —
Beyond the clouds, in the clear sky
    Close by some quiet star —
Could you not fancy there might be
A home, Beloved, for you and me?"

"If there were such a home, my Friend,
    Truly prepared for us,
Full of palm-branches or of crowns,
    Sun-gemmed and glorious,
How should we reach it? Let us cease
From longing; let us be at peace."

"The nightingale sang yestereve;
    A sweet song singeth she,
Most sad and without any hope,
    And full of memory;
But still methought it seemed to speak
To me of home, and bid me seek."

"The nightingale ceased ere the morn:
    Her heart could not contain
The passion of her song, but burst
    With the loud throbbing pain.
Now she hath rest which is the best,
And now I too would be at rest."

"Last night I watched the mounting moon:
   Her glory was too pale
To shine through the black heavy clouds
   That wrapt her like a veil;
And yet with patience she passed through
The mists, and reached the depths of blue."

"And when the road was travelled o'er
   And when the goal was won,
A little while and all her light
   Was swallowed by the sun:
The weary moon must seek again, —
Even so our search would be in vain."

"Yet seek with me. And if our way
   Be long and troublesome,
And if our noon be hot until
   The chilly shadows come
Of evening, — till those shadows flee
In dawn, think, Love, it is with me."

"Nay seek alone: I am no mate
   For such as you, in truth:
My heart is old before its time;
   Yours yet is in its youth:
This home with pleasures girt about
Seek you, for I am wearied out."

6 *October* 1849.

SEEKING REST

MY Mother said: "The child is changed
    That used to be so still;
All the day long she sings and sings,
    And seems to think no ill;
She laughs as if some inward joy
    Her heart would overfill."

My Sisters said: " Now prythee tell
    Thy secret unto us:
Let us rejoice with thee; for all
    Is surely prosperous,
Thou art so merry: tell us, Sweet:
    We had not used thee thus."

My Mother says: "What ails the child
    Lately so blythe of cheer?
Art sick or sorry? Nay, it is
    The winter of the year;
Wait till the Springtime comes again,
    And the sweet flowers appear."

My Sisters say: "Come, sit with us,
    That we may weep with thee:
Show us thy grief that we may grieve
    Yea haply, if we see
Thy sorrow, we may ease it; but
    Shall share it certainly."

How should I share my pain, who kept
My pleasure all my own?
My Spring will never come again;
My pretty flowers have blown
For the last time; I can but sit
And think and weep alone.

10 *October* 1849.

TWO THOUGHTS OF DEATH

I

HER heart that loved me once is rottenness
Now and corruption; and her life is dead
That was to have been one with mine, she said.
The earth must lie with such a cruel stress
On eyes whereon the white lids used to press;
Foul worms fill up her mouth so sweet and red;
Foul worms are underneath her graceful head;
Yet these, being born of her from nothingness,
These worms are certainly flesh of her flesh. —
How is it that the grass is rank and green
And the dew-dropping rose is brave and fresh
Above what was so sweeter far than they?
Even as her beauty hath passed quite away,
Theirs too shall be as though it had not been.

II

So I said underneath the dusky trees:
   But, because still I loved her memory,
   I stooped to pluck a pale anemone,
And lo my hand lighted upon heartsease
Not fully blown: while with new life from these
   Fluttered a starry moth that rapidly
   Rose toward the sun: sunlighted flashed on me
Its wings that seemed to throb like heart-pulses.
Far far away it flew, far out of sight, —
   From earth and flowers of earth it passed away
As though it flew straight up into the light.
   Then my heart answered me: Thou fool, to say
   That she is dead whose night is turned to day,
And no more shall her day turn back to night.

   16 *March* 1850.

THREE MOMENTS

THE Child said: " Pretty bird,
   Come back and play with me."
The Bird said: " It is in vain,
   For I am free.
I am free, I will not stay,
But will fly far away,
In the woods to sing and play,
   Far away, far away."
The Child sought her Mother:
" I have lost my bird," said she,

Weeping bitterly.
But the Mother made her answer,
Half sighing pityingly,
Half smiling cheerily:
"Though thy bird come nevermore,
    Do not weep;
Find another playfellow
    Child, and keep
Tears for future pain more deep."

"Sweet rose, do not wither,"
    The Girl said.
But a blight had touched its heart
And it drooped its crimson head.
In the morning it had opened
    Full of life and bloom,
But the leaves fell one by one
    Till the twilight gloom.
One by one the leaves fell
By summer winds blown from their stem;
They fell upon the dewy earth
Which nourished once now tainted them.
Again the young Girl wept
And sought her Mother's ear:
"My rose is dead so full of grace,
The very rose I meant to place
    In the wreath that I wear."
"Nay, never weep for such as this,"
    The Mother answered her:
"But weave another crown, less fair

Perhaps, but fitter for thy hair.
And keep thy tears," the Mother said,
  " For something heavier."

The Woman knelt, but did not pray
Nor weep nor cry; she only said:
" Not this, not this ! " and clasped her hands
Against her heart, and bowed her head,
While the great struggle shook the bed.
" Not this, not this ! " tears did not fall;
" Not this ! " it was all
She could say; no sobs would come;
The mortal grief was almost dumb. —
At length when it was over, when
She knew it was and would be so,
She cried: " O Mother, where are they,
  The tears that used to flow
So easily? One single drop
Might save my reason now, or stop
My heart from breaking. Blessed tears
  Wasted in former years ! "
Then the grave Mother made reply:
" O Daughter mine, be of good cheer,
Rejoicing thou canst shed no tear.
Thy pain is almost over now.
Once more thy heart shall throb with pain,
But then shall never throb again.
Oh happy thou who canst not weep,
  Oh happy thou ! "

23 *March* 1850.

IS AND WAS

SHE was whiter than the ermine
    That half shadowed neck and hand,
And her tresses were more golden
    Than their golden band;
Snowy ostrich plumes she wore;
Yet I almost loved her more
In the simple time before.

Then she plucked the stately lilies
Knowing not she was more fair,
And she listened to the skylark
    In the morning air.
Then, a kerchief all her crown,
She looked for the acorns brown,
Bent their bough, and shook them down.

Then she thought of Christmas holly
And of Maybloom in sweet May;
Then she loved to pick the cherries
    And to turn the hay.
She was humble then and meek,
And the blush upon her cheek
Told of much she could not speak.

Now she is a noble lady
With calm voice not over loud;
Very courteous in her action,
   Yet you think her proud;
Much too haughty to affect;
Too indifferent to direct
Or be angry or suspect;
Doing all from self-respect.

Spring 1850.

SONG

WE buried her among the flowers
   At falling of the leaf,
And choked back all our tears; her joy
   Could never be our grief.

She lies among the living flowers
   And grass, the only thing
That perishes;— or is it that
   Our Autumn was her Spring?

Doubtless, if we could see her face,
   The smile is settled there
Which almost broke our hearts when last
   We knelt by her in prayer;

When, with tired eyes and failing breath
    And hands crossed on her breast,
Perhaps she saw her Guardian spread
    His wings above her rest.

So she sleeps hidden in the flowers;
    But yet a little while,
And we shall see her wake and rise,
    Fair, with the self-same smile.

14 *May* 1850.

ANNIE

ANNIE is fairer than her kith
    And kinder than her kin:
Her eyes are like the open heaven
    Holy and pure from sin:
Her heart is like an ordered house
    Good fairies harbour in:
Oh happy he who wins the love
    That I can never win!

Her sisters stand as hyacinths
    Around the perfect rose:
They bloom and open to the full,
    My bud will scarce unclose.
They are for every butterfly
    That comes and sips and goes;
My bud hides in the tender green
    Most sweet and hardly shows.

Oh cruel kindness in soft eyes
    That are no more than kind,
On which I gaze my heart away
    Till the tears make me blind!
How is it others find the way
    That I can never find
To make her laugh that sweetest laugh
    Which leaves all else behind?

Her hair is like the golden corn
    A low wind breathes upon:
Or like the golden harvest-moon
    When all the mists are gone:
Or like a stream with golden sands
    On which the sun has shone
Day after day in summertime
    Ere autumn leaves are wan.

I will not tell her that I love,
    Lest she should turn away
With sorrow in her tender heart
    Which now is light and gay.
I will not tell her that I love,
    Lest she should turn and say
That we must meet no more again
    For many a weary day.

26 *September* 1850.

A DIRGE

SHE was as sweet as violets in the Spring,
As fair as any rose in Summertime:
But frail are roses in their prime
And violets in their blossoming.
    Even so was she:
    And now she lies,
The earth upon her fast-closed eyes,
Dead in the darkness silently.

The sweet Spring violets never bud again,
The roses bloom and perish in a morn:
They see no second quickening lying lorn:
    Their beauty dies as though in vain.
        Must she die so
        For evermore,
    Cold as the sand upon the shore,
    As passionless for joy and woe?—

Nay she is worth much more than flowers that fade,
And yet shall be made fair with purple fruit:
    Branch of the Living Vine, whose Root
    From all eternity is laid.
        Another Sun
        Than this of ours
    Has withered up indeed her flowers
    But ripened her grapes every one.

18 *January* 1851.

SONG

IT is not for her even brow
   And shining yellow hair,
But it is for her tender eyes
   I think my love so fair:
Her tell-tale eyes that smile and weep
As frankly as they wake and sleep.

It is not for her rounded cheek
   I love and fain would win,
But it is for the blush that comes
   Straight from the heart within:
The honest blush of maiden shame
That blushes without thought of blame.

So in my dreams I never hear
   Her song, although she sings
As if a choir of spirits swept
   From earth with throbbing wings:
I only hear the simple voice
Whose love makes many hearts rejoice.

1851.

A FAIR WORLD THOUGH A FALLEN

YOU tell me that the world is fair, in spite,
   Of the old Fall; and that I should not turn
So to the grave, and let my spirit yearn
After the quiet of the long last night.
Have I then shut mine eyes against the light,
   Grief-deafened lest my spirit should discern?
   Yet how could I keep silence when I burn?
And who can give me comfort?—Hear the right.
Have patience with the weak and sick at heart:
   Bind up the wounded with a tender touch,
      Comfort the sad, tear-blinded as they go:—
For, though I failed to choose the better part,
      Were it a less unutterable woe
   If we should come to love this world too much?

30 *August* 1851.

BOOKS IN THE RUNNING BROOKS

" IT is enough, enough," one said,
   At play among the flowers:
" I spy a rose upon the thorn,
   A rainbow in the showers;
I hear a merry chime of bells
   Ring out the passing hours."

Soft springs the fountain
From the daisied ground,
Softly falling on the moss
Without a sound.

"It is enough," she said, and fixed
Calm eyes upon the sky:
"I watch a flitting tender cloud
Just like a dove go by;
A lark is rising from the grass,
A wren is building nigh."
Softly the fountain
Threads its silver way,
Screened by the scented bloom
Of whitest May.

"Enough?" she whispered to herself,
As doubting: "Is it so?
Enough to wear the roses fair,
O sweetest flowers that blow?
Oh yes, it surely is enough —
My happy home below!"
A shadow stretcheth
From the hither shore:
The waters darken
More and more and more.

"It is enough," she says; but with
A listless weary moan:
"Enough," if mixing with her friends:
"Enough," if left alone;

But to herself: "Not yet enough
This suffering, to atone?"
The cold black waters
Seem to stagnate there,
Without a single wave
Or breath of air.

And now she says: "It is enough,"
Half languid and half stirred:
"Enough," to silence and to sound,
Thorn, blossom, soaring bird:
"Enough," she says; but with a lack
Of something in the word.
Defiled and turbid
See the waters pass,
Half light, half shadow,
Struggling through the grass.

Ah will it ever dawn, that day
When, calm for good or ill,
Her heart shall say: "It is enough,
For Thou art with me still;
It is enough, O LORD my GOD,
Thine only blessed Will"?
Then shall the fountain sing
And flow to rest,
Clear as the sun-track
To the purple West.

26 *August* 1852.

THE SUMMER IS ENDED

WREATHE no more lilies in my hair,
 For I am dying, Sister sweet:
Or, if you will for the last time
 Indeed, why make me fair
 Once for my winding-sheet.

Pluck no more roses for my breast,
 For I like them fade in my prime:
Or, if you will, why pluck them still,
 That they may share my rest
 Once more for the last time.

Weep not for me when I am gone,
 Dear tender one, but hope and smile:
Or, if you cannot choose but weep,
 A little while weep on,
 Only a little while.

11 *September* 1852.

AFTER ALL

"I THOUGHT your search was over." — "So I thought."
"But you are seeking still." — "Yes, even so:
Still seeking in mine own despite below
That which in heaven alone is found unsought:
Still spending for that thing which is not bought."

"Then chase no more this shifting empty show." —
"Amen : so bid a drowning man forego
The straw he clutches : will he so be taught?
You have a home where peace broods like a dove,
    Screened from the weary world's loud discontent :
You have home here : you wait for home above.
    I must unlearn the pleasant ways I went :
Must learn another hope, another love,
    And sigh indeed for home in banishment."

24 *October* 1852.

FROM THE ANTIQUE

THE wind shall lull us yet,
    The flowers shall spring above us :
And those who hate forget,
    And those forget who love us.

The pulse of hope shall cease,
    Of joy and of regretting :
We twain shall sleep in peace,
    Forgotten and forgetting.

For us no sun shall rise,
    Nor wind rejoice, nor river,
Where we with fast-closed eyes
    Shall sleep and sleep for ever.

10 *December* 1852.

TO WHAT PURPOSE IS THIS WASTE?

A WINDY shell singing upon the shore :
   A lily budding in a desert place,
      Blooming alone
      With no companion
To praise its perfect perfume and its grace :
A rose crimson and blushing at the core,
Hedged-in with thorns behind it and before :
     A fountain in the grass,
     Whose shadowy waters pass
Only to nourish birds and furnish food
    For squirrels of the wood :
An oak deep in the forest's heart, the house
    Of black-eyed tiny mouse :
Its strong roots, fit for fuel, roofing in
   The hoarded nuts, acorns, and grains of wheat—
   Shutting them from the wind and scorching heat,
And sheltering them when the rains begin :

A precious pearl deep-buried in the sea
    Where none save fishes be :
    The fullest merriest note
For which the skylark strains his silver throat,
   Heard only in the sky
   By other birds that fitfully
   Chase one another as they fly :

TO WHAT PURPOSE IS THIS WASTE?

The ripest plum down-tumbled to the ground
By southern winds most musical of sound,
   But by no thirsty traveller found :
Honey of wild bees in their ordered cells
   Stored, not for human mouths to taste : —
I said smiling superior down : What waste
    Of good, where no man dwells !

This I said on a pleasant day in June
Before the sun had set, though a white moon
   Already flaked the quiet blue
    Which not a star looked through.
But still the air was warm, and drowsily
    It blew into my face :
So, since that same day I had wandered deep
Into the country, I sought out a place
    For rest beneath a tree,
And very soon forgot myself in sleep :
Not so mine own words had forgotten me.
   Mine eyes were open to behold
    All hidden things,
And mine ears heard all secret whisperings :
   So my proud tongue, that had been bold
    To carp and to reprove,
Was silenced by the force of utter Love.

All voices of all things inanimate
Join with the song of Angels and the song
   Of blessed spirits, chiming with
Their Hallelujahs. One wind wakeneth

Across the sleeping sea, crisping along
The waves, and brushes through the great
Forests and tangled hedges, and calls out
    Of rivers a clear sound,
And makes the ripe corn rustle on the ground,
    And murmurs in a shell:
        Till all their voices swell
    Above the clouds in one loud hymn
    Joining the song of Seraphim,
Or like pure incense circle roundabout
The walls of heaven, or like a well-spring rise
    In shady Paradise.

A lily blossoming unseen
Holds honey in its silver cup
    Whereon a bee may sup,
Till being full she takes the rest
And stores it in her waxen nest:
While the fair blossom lifted up
On its one stately stem of green
Is type of her the Undefiled,
Arrayed in white, whose eyes are mild
As a white dove's, whose garment is
Blood-cleansed from all impurities
    And earthly taints,
Her robe the righteousness of Saints.

    And other eyes than ours
    Were made to look on flowers,
    Eyes of small birds and insects small:

64 TO WHAT PURPOSE IS THIS WASTE?

The deep sun-blushing rose
Round which the prickles close
Opens her bosom to them all.
The tiniest living thing
That soars on feathered wing,
Or crawls among the long grass out of sight,
Has just as good a right
To its appointed portion of delight
As any King.

Why should we grudge a hidden water-stream
To birds and squirrels while we have enough?
As if a nightingale should cease to sing
Lest we should hear, or finch leafed out of sight
Warbling its fill in summer light:
As if sweet violets in the Spring
Should cease to blow, for fear our path should seem
Less weary or less rough.

So every oak that stands a house
For skilful mouse
And year by year renews its strength,
Shakes acorns from a hundred boughs
Which shall be oaks at length.

Who hath weighed the waters and shall say
What is hidden in the depths from day?
Pearls and precious stones and golden sands,
Wondrous weeds and blossoms rare,
Kept back from human hands,
But good and fair,

A silent praise as pain is silent prayer.
A hymn and incense rising toward the skies,
    As our whole life should rise :
An offering without stint from earth below,
    Which Love accepteth so.

Thus is it with a warbling bird,
With fruit bloom-ripe and full of seed,
With honey which the wild bees draw
From flowers, and store for future need
    By a perpetual law.
We want the faith that hath not seen
Indeed, but hath believed His truth
Who witnessed that His work was good :
So we pass cold to age from youth.
Alas for us, for we have heard
And known, but have not understood.

O earth, earth, earth, thou yet shalt bow
Who art so fair and lifted up,
Thou yet shalt drain the bitter cup.
Men's eyes that wait upon thee now,
All eyes shall see thee lost and mean,
Exposed and valued at thy worth,
While thou shalt stand ashamed and dumb.—
Ah when the Son of Man shall come,
Shall He find faith upon the earth?

22 January 1853.

NEXT OF KIN

THE shadows gather round me, while you are
in the sun :
My day is almost ended, but yours is just begun :
The winds are singing to us both and the streams are
singing still,
And they fill your heart with music, but mine they
cannot fill.

Your home is built in sunlight, mine in another
day :
Your home is close at hand, sweet friend, but mine
is far away :
Your bark is in the haven where you fain would be :
I must launch out into the deep, across the unknown
sea.

You, white as dove or lily or spirit of the light :
I, stained and cold and glad to hide in the cold
dark night :
You, joy to many a loving heart and light to many
eyes :
I, lonely in the knowledge earth is full of vanities.

Yet when your day is over, as mine is nearly done,
And when your race is finished, as mine is almost
run.

You, like me, shall cross your hands and bow your
    graceful head :
Yea, we twain shall sleep together in an equal bed.

21 *February* 1853.

PORTRAITS

A N easy lazy length of limb,
    Dark eyes and features from the South,
A short-legged meditative pipe
    Set in a supercilious mouth :
Ink and a pen and papers laid
    Down on a table for the night,
Beside a semi-dozing man
    Who wakes to go to bed by light.

. . . .

A pair of brothers brotherly,
    Unlike and yet how much the same
In heart and high-toned intellect,
    In face and bearing, hope and aim :
Friends of the selfsame treasured friends
    And of one home the dear delight,
Beloved of many a loving heart,
    And cherished both in mine, Good-night.

9 *May* 1853.

WHAT?

STRENGTHENING as secret manna,
   Fostering as clouds above,
  Kind as a hovering dove,
  Full as a plenteous river,
Our glory and our banner
  For ever and for ever.

  Dear as a dying cadence
Of music in the drowsy night:
  Fair as the flowers which maidens
  Pluck for an hour's delight,
  And then forget them quite.

  Gay as a cowslip-meadow
    Fresh opening to the sun
    When new day is begun:
  Soft as a sunny shadow
    When day is almost done.

  Glorious as purple twilight,
    Pleasant as budding tree,
  Untouched as any islet
    Shrined in an unknown sea:
Sweet as a fragrant rose amid the dew:—
  As sweet, as fruitless too.

A bitter dream to wake from,
But oh how pleasant while we dream !
A poisoned fount to take from,
But oh how sweet the stream !

May 1853.

NEAR THE STYX

IN my cottage near the Styx
   Co. and Charon still combine
Us to ferry o'er like bricks
In a boat of chaste design.
Cerberus, thou triple fair,
Distance doth thy charms impair :
Let the passage give to us
Charon, Co., and Cerberus.

Chorus

Now the passage gives us to
Charon, Cerberus, and Co.

June 1853 — Frome Selwood.

A PAUSE

THEY made the chamber sweet with flowers and
    leaves,
  And the bed sweet with flowers on which I lay;
  While my soul, love-bound, loitered on its way.
I did not hear the birds about the eaves,
Nor hear the reapers talk among the sheaves:
  Only my soul kept watch from day to day,
  My thirsty soul kept watch for one away:—
Perhaps he loves, I thought, remembers, grieves.
At length there came a step upon the stair,
  Upon the lock the old familiar hand:
Then first my spirit seemed to scent the air
  Of Paradise; then first the tardy sand
Of time ran golden; and I felt my hair
  Put on a glory, and my soul expand.

10 *June* 1853.

HOLY INNOCENTS

SLEEP, little Baby, sleep;
  The holy Angels love thee,
And guard thy bed, and keep
  A blessed watch above thee.
No spirit can come near
  Nor evil beast to harm thee:

Sleep, Sweet, devoid of fear
  Where nothing need alarm thee.

The Love which doth not sleep,
  The eternal Arms surround thee:
The Shepherd of the sheep
  In perfect love hath found thee.
Sleep through the holy night,
  Christ-kept from snare and sorrow,
Until thou wake to light
  And love and warmth to-morrow.

1 *July* 1853.

SEASONS

IN Springtime when the leaves are young,
  Clear dewdrops gleam like jewels, hung
On boughs the fair birds roost among.

When Summer comes with sweet unrest,
Birds weary of their mother's breast,
And look abroad and leave the nest.

In Autumn ere the waters freeze,
The swallows fly across the seas: —
If we could fly away with these!

In Winter when the birds are gone,
The sun himself looks starved and wan,
And starved the snow he shines upon.

September 1853.

BURIED

THOU sleepest where the lilies fade,
    Thou dwellest where the lilies fade not:
Sweet, when thine earthly part decayed
    Thy heavenly part decayed not.

Thou dwellest where the roses blow,
    The crimson roses bud and blossom:
While on thine eyes is heaped the snow —
    The snow upon thy bosom.

1853.

A WISH

I WISH I were a little bird
    That out of sight doth soar;
I wish I were a song once heard
    But often pondered o'er,
Or shadow of a lily stirred
    By wind upon the floor,
Or echo of a loving word
    Worth all that went before,
Or memory of a hope deferred
    That springs again no more.

1853.

TWO PARTED

"SING of a love lost and forgotten,
    Sing of a joy finished and o'er,
Sing of a heart core-cold and rotten,
    Sing of a hope springing no more."
    "Sigh for a heart aching and sore."

"I was most true and my own love betrayed me,
    I was most true and she would none of me.
Was it the cry of the world that dismayed thee?
    Love, I had bearded the wide world for thee."
    "Hark to the sorrowful sound of the sea."

"Still in my dreams she comes tender and gracious,
    Still in my dreams love looks out of her eyes:
Oh that the love of a dream were veracious,
    Or that thus dreaming I might not arise!"
    "Oh for the silence that stilleth all sighs!"
1853.

FOR ROSALINE'S ALBUM

DO you hear the low winds singing,
    And streams singing on their bed? —
Very distant bells are ringing
    In a chapel for the dead : —
    Death-pale better than life-red.

Mother, come to me in rest,
    And bring little May to see.
Shall I bid no other guest?
Seven slow nights have passed away
Over my forgotten clay :
    None must come save you and she.
1853.

AUTUMN

CARE flieth,
    Hope and Fear together :
Love dieth
In the Autumn weather.

    For a friend
Even Care is pleasant :
    When Fear doth end
Hope is no more present :
Autumn silences the turtle-dove : —
    In blank Autumn who could speak of love?
1853.

SEASONS

CROCUSES and snowdrops wither,
    Violets, primroses together,
Fading with the fading Spring
Before a fuller blossoming.

O sweet Summer, pass not soon,
Stay awhile the harvest-moon:
O sweetest Summer, do not go,
For Autumn's next and next the snow.

When Autumn comes the days are drear,
It is the downfall of the year:
We heed the wind and falling leaf
More than the golden harvest-sheaf.

Dreary Winter come at last:
Come quickly, so be quickly past:
Dusk and sluggish Winter wane
Till Spring and sunlight dawn again.

7 *December* 1853.

BALLAD

"SOFT white lamb in the daisy meadow,
    Come hither and play with me,
For I am lonesome and I am tired
    Underneath the apple tree."

"There's your husband if you are lonesome, lady,
    And your bed if you want for rest:
And your baby for a playfellow
    With a soft hand for your breast."

"Fair white dove in the sunshine,
    Perched on the ashen bough,
Come and perch by me and coo to me
    While the buds are blowing now."

"I must keep my nestlings warm, lady,
    Underneath my downy breast:
There's your baby to coo and crow to you
    While I brood upon my nest."

"Faint white rose, come lie on my heart,
    Come lie there with your thorn:
For I'll be dead at the vesper-bell
    And buried the morrow morn."

"There's blood on your lily breast, lady,
    Like roses when they blow,
And there's blood upon your little hand
    That should be white as snow:
I will stay amid my fellows
    Where the lilies grow."

"But it's oh my own own little babe
    That I had you here to kiss,
And to comfort me in the strange next world
    Though I slighted you so in this."

"You shall kiss both cheek and chin, mother,
    And kiss me between the eyes,
Or ever the moon is on her way
    And the pleasant stars arise :
You shall kiss and kiss your fill, mother,
    In the nest of Paradise."

7 *January* 1854.

A SOUL

SHE stands as pale as Parian statues stand ;
    Like Cleopatra when she turned at bay,
And felt her strength above the Roman sway,
And felt the aspic writhing in her hand.
Her face is steadfast toward the shadowy land,
    For dim beyond it looms the land of day :
    Her feet are steadfast, all the arduous way
That foot-track doth not waver on the sand.
She stands there like a beacon through the night,
    A pale clear beacon where the storm-drift is—
She stands alone, a wonder deathly-white :
She stands there patient nerved with inner might,
    Indomitable in her feebleness,
Her face and will athirst against the light.

7 *February* 1854.

FROM THE ANTIQUE

IT'S a weary life, it is, she said :—
Doubly blank in a woman's lot :
I wish and I wish I were a man :
Or, better than any being, were not :

Were nothing at all in all the world,
Not a body and not a soul :
Not so much as a grain of dust
Or drop of water from pole to pole.

Still the world would wag on the same,
Still the seasons go and come :
Blossoms bloom as in days of old,
Cherries ripen and wild bees hum.

None would miss me in all the world,
How much less would care or weep :
I should be nothing, while all the rest
Would wake and weary and fall asleep.

28 June 1854

RESTIVE

I THOUGHT to deal the death-stroke at a blow:
To give all, once for all, but never more:—
Then sit to hear the low waves fret the shore,
    Or watch the silent snow.

"Oh rest," I thought, "in silence and the dark:
Oh rest, if nothing else, from head to feet:
Though I may see no more the poppied wheat,
    Or sunny soaring lark.

"These chimes are slow, but surely strike at last:
This sand is slow, but surely droppeth through:
And much there is to suffer, much to do,
    Before the time be past.

"So will I labour, but will not rejoice:
Will do and bear, but will not hope again.
Gone dead alike to pulses of quick pain
    And pleasure's counterpoise."

I said so in my heart: and so I thought
My life would lapse, a tedious monotone:
I thought to shut myself and dwell alone
    Unseeking and unsought:

But first I tired, and then my care grew slack,
Till my heart dreamed, and maybe wandered too: —
I felt the sunshine glow again, and knew
   The swallow on its track:

All birds awoke to building in the leaves,
All buds awoke to fulness and sweet scent:
Ah too my heart woke unawares, intent
   On fruitful harvest-sheaves..

Full pulse of life, that I had deemed was dead;
Full throb of youth, that I had deemed at rest.
Alas I cannot build myself a nest,
   I cannot crown my head

With royal purple blossoms for the feast,
Nor flush with laughter, nor exult in song: —
These joys may drift, as time now drifts along;
   And cease, as once they ceased.

I may pursue, and yet may not attain,
Athirst and panting all the days I live:
Or seem to hold, yet nerve myself to give
   What once I gave, again.

25 July 1854.

LONG LOOKED FOR

WHEN the eye hardly sees,
    And the pulse hardly stirs,
And the heart would scarcely quicken
    Though the voice were hers:
Then the longing wasting fever
    Will be almost past:
Sleep indeed come back again,
    And peace at last.

    Not till then, dear friends,
Not till then, most like, most dear,
    The dove will fold its wings
        To settle here.
    Then to all her coldness
    I also shall be cold;
Then I also have forgotten
    Our happy love of old.

    Close mine eyes with care,
Cross my hands upon my breast,
    Let shadows and full silence
        Tell of rest:
For she yet may look upon me
    Too proud to speak, but know
One heart less loves her in the world
    Than loved her long ago.

Strew flowers upon the bed
And flowers upon the floor,
Let all be sweet and comely
When she stands at the door:
Fair as a bridal chamber
For her to come into,
When the sunny day is over
At falling of the dew.

If she comes, watch her not,
But careless turn aside:
She may weep if left alone
With her beauty and her pride:
She may pluck a leaf perhaps
Or a languid violet
When life and love are finished
And even I forget.

12 *August* 1854.

LISTENING

SHE listened like a cushat dove
   That listens to its mate alone:
She listened like a cushat dove
   That loves but only one.

Not fair as men would reckon fair,
Nor noble as they count the line:
Only as graceful as a bough,
   And tendrils of the vine:

Only as noble as sweet Eve
Your ancestress and mine.

And downcast were her dovelike eyes
And downcast was her tender cheek;
Her pulses fluttered like a dove
To hear him speak.

October 1854.

THE LAST LOOK

HER face was like an opening rose,
   So bright to look upon:
But now it is like fallen snows,
   As cold, as dead, as wan.

Heaven lit with stars is more like her
   Than is this empty crust:
Deaf, dumb, and blind, it cannot stir,
   But crumbles back to dust.

No flower be taken from her bed
   For me, no lock be shorn:
I give her up, the early dead,
   The dead, the newly born.

If I remember her, no need
   Of formal tokens set;
Of hollow token-lies indeed
   No need, if I forget.

23 *March* 1855.

I HAVE A MESSAGE UNTO THEE

(WRITTEN IN SICKNESS)

GREEN sprout the grasses,
　　Red blooms the mossy rose,
Blue nods the harebell
Where purple heather blows:
The water-lily, silver white,
　Is living fair as light:

Sweet jasmine-branches trail
A dusky starry veil:
Each goodly is to see,
Comely in its degree:
I only I, alas that this should be,
Am ruinously pale.

New year renews the grasses,
The crimson rose renews,
Brings up the breezy bluebell,
Refreshes heath with dews:
Then water-lilies ever
Bud fresh upon the river:
Then jasmine lights its star
And spreads its arms afar:

I only in my spring
Can neither bud nor sing:
I find not honey but a sting
Though fair the blossoms are.

For me no downy grasses,
For me no blossoms pluck:
But leave them for the breezes,
For honey-bees to suck,
For childish hands to pull
And pile their baskets full:
I will not have a crown
That soon must be laid down:
Trust me: I cannot care
A withering crown to wear,
I who may be immortally made fair
Where autumn turns not brown.

Spring, summer, autumn,
Winter, all will pass,
  With tender blossoms
And with fruitful grass.
  Sweet days of yore
Will pass to come no more,
  Sweet perfumes fly,
Buds languish and go by:
Oh bloom that cannot last,
Oh blossoms quite gone past,
I yet shall feast when you shall fast,
And live when you shall die.

Your work-day fully ended,
Your pleasant task being done,
You shall finish with the stars,
  The moon and setting sun.
You and these and time
Shall end with the last chime, —
For earthly solace given,
But needed not in heaven;
Needed not perhaps
Through the eternal lapse.
Or else, all signs fulfilled,
What you foreshow may yield
Delights through heaven's own harvest field
  With undecaying saps.

Young girls wear flowers,
Young brides a flowery wreath:
  But next we plant them
  In garden-plots of death.
Whose sleep is best? —
The maiden's curtained rest,
Or bride's whose hoped-for sweet
May yet outstrip her feet? —
Ah what are such as these
To death's sufficing ease?
How long and deep that slumber is
  Where night and morning meet!

  Dear are the blossoms
  For bride's or maiden's head,

But dearer planted
Around our happy dead.
Those mind us of decay
And joys that slip away:
These preach to us perfection
And endless resurrection.
We make our graveyards fair
For spirit-like birds of air:
For Angels, may be, finding there
Lost Eden's own delection.

A blessing on the flowers
That God has made so good,
From crops of jealous gardens
To wildlings of a wood.
They show us symbols deep
Of how to sow and reap:
They teach us lessons plain
Of patient harvest-gain.
They still are telling of
God's unimagined love:—
"Oh gift," they say, "all gifts above,
Shall it be given in vain?—

"Better you had not seen us
But shared the blind man's night,
Better you had not scented
Our incense of delight,
Than only plucked to scorn
The rosebud for its thorn:

Not so the instinctive thrush
Hymns in a holly-bush.
Be wise betimes, and with the bee
Suck sweets from prickly tree,
To last when earth's are flown:
So God well pleased will own
Your work, and bless not time alone
But ripe eternity."

26 *March* 1855.

COBWEBS

IT is a land with neither night nor day,
Nor heat nor cold, nor any wind nor rain,
Nor hills nor valleys: but one even plain
Stretches through long unbroken miles away,
While through the sluggish air a twilight grey
Broodeth: no moons or seasons wax and wane,
No ebb and flow are there along the main,
No bud-time, no leaf-falling, there for aye:—
No ripple on the sea, no shifting sand,
No beat of wings to stir the stagnant space:
No pulse of life through all the loveless land
And loveless sea; no trace of days before,
No guarded home, no toil-won resting-place,
No future hope, no fear for evermore.

October 1855.

AN AFTER-THOUGHT

OH lost garden Paradise! —
   Were the roses redder there
Than they blossom otherwhere?
Was the night's delicious shade
   More intensely star-inlaid?
Who can tell what memories
Of lost beloved Paradise
Saddened Eve with sleepless eyes?

Fair first mother lulled to rest
In a choicer garden-nest,
Curtained with a softer shading
Than thy tenderest child is laid in, —
Was the sundawn brighter far
Than our daily sundawns are?
Was that love, first love of all,
   Warmer, deeper, better worth
   Than has warmed poor hearts of earth
Since the utter ruinous fall?

Ah supremely happy once,
   Ah supremely broken-hearted
   When her tender feet departed
   From the accustomed paths of peace:
Catching Angel orisons
For the last last time of all,

Shedding tears that would not cease
   For the bitter fall.

Yet the accustomed hand for leading,
Yet the accustomed heart for love :
Sure she kept one part of Eden
   Angels could not strip her of.
Sure the fiery messenger
   Kindling for his outraged Lord,
      Willing with the perfect Will,
   Yet rejoiced the flaming sword,
      Chastening sore but sparing still,
Shut her treasure out with her.

What became of Paradise?
   Did the cedars droop at all
   (Springtide hastening to the fall)
   Missing the beloved hand —
   Or did their green perfection stand
Unmoved beneath the perfect skies? —
Paradise was rapt on high,
   It lies before the gate of Heaven : —
   Eve now slumbers there forgiven,
   Slumbers Rachel comforted,
   Slumber all the blessed dead
Of days and months and years gone by,
A solemn swelling company.

They wait for us beneath the trees
Of Paradise, that lap of ease :

They wait for us, till God shall please.
Oh come the day of death, that day
Of rest which cannot pass away!
When the last work is wrought, the last
Pang of pain is felt and past,
And the blessed door made fast.

18 *December* 1855.

TO THE END

THERE are lilies for her sisters —
  (Who so cold as they?) —
And heartsease for one I must not name
  When I am far away.
I shall pluck the lady lilies
  And fancy all the rest:
I shall pluck the bright-eyed heartsease
  For her sake I love the best:
As I wander on with weary feet
  Toward the twilight shadowy west.

O bird that flyest eastward
  Unto that sunny land,
Oh wilt thou light on lilies white
  Beside her whiter hand?
Soft summer wind that breathest
  Of perfumes and sweet spice,

TO THE END

Ah tell her what I dare not tell
Of watchful waiting eyes,
Of love that yet may meet again
In distant Paradise.

I go from earth to heaven
A dim uncertain road,
A houseless pilgrim through the world
Unto a sure abode:
While evermore an Angel
Goes with me day and night,
A ministering spirit
From the land of light,
My holy fellow-servant sent
To guide my steps aright.

I wonder if the Angels
Love with such love as ours,
If for each other's sake they pluck
And keep eternal flowers.
Alone I am and weary,
Alone yet not alone:
Her soul talks with me by the way
From tedious stone to stone,
A blessed Angel treads with me
The awful paths unknown.

When will the long road end in rest,
The sick bird perch and brood?
When will my Guardian fold his wings
At rest in the finished good?—

Lulling, lulling me off to sleep:
  While Death's strong hand doth roll
  My sins behind his back,
  And my life up like a scroll,
Till through sleep I hear kind Angels
  Rejoicing at the goal.

If her spirit went before me
  Up from night to day,
It would pass me like the lightning
  That kindles on its way.
I should feel it like the lightning
  Flashing fresh from Heaven:
I should long for Heaven sevenfold more,
  Yea and sevenfold seven:
Should pray as I have not prayed before,
  And strive as I have not striven.

She will learn new love in Heaven,
  Who is so full of love;
She will learn new depths of tenderness
  Who is tender like a dove.
  Her heart will no more sorrow,
  Her eyes will weep no more:
Yet it may be she will yearn
  And look back from far before:
Lingering on the golden threshold
  And leaning from the door.

18 *December* 1855.

MAY

" SWEET Life is dead." — " Not so :
I meet him day by day,
Where bluest fountains flow
And trees are white as snow,
For it is time of May.
Even now from long ago
He will not say me nay,
He is most fair to see :
And if I wander forth, I know
He wanders forth with me."

" But Life is dead to me :
The worn-out year was failing,
West winds took up a wailing
To watch his funeral :
Bare poplars shivered tall
And lank vines stretched to see.
'Twixt him and me a wall
Was frozen of earth-like stone
With brambles overgrown :
Chill darkness wrapped him like a pall
And I am left alone."

" How can you call him dead?
He buds out everywhere :

In every hedgerow rank,
On every mossgrown bank,
I find him here and there.
He crowns my willing head
With May-flowers white and red,
He rears my tender heartsease-bed :
He makes my branch to bud and bear,
And blossoms where I tread."

31 *December* 1855.

BY THE WATER

THERE are rivers lapsing down
    Lily-laden to the sea :
Every lily is a boat
    For bees, one, two, or three :
I wish there were a fairy boat
    For you, my friend, and me.

And if there were a fairy boat
    And if the river bore us,
We should not care for all the past
    Nor all that lies before us,
Not for the hopes that buoyed us once
    Not for the fears that tore us.

We would rock upon the river
    Scarcely floating by,

Rocking, rocking like the lilies,
   You, my friend, and I:
Rocking like the stately lilies
   Beneath the statelier sky.

But ah where is that river
   Whose hyacinth banks descend
Down to the sweeter lilies
   Till soft their shadows blend
Into a watery twilight? —
   And ah where is my friend?

7 February 1856.

A CHILLY NIGHT

I ROSE at the dead of night,
   And went to the lattice alone
To look for my Mother's ghost
   Where the ghostly moonlight shone.

My friends had failed one by one,
   Middle-aged, young, and old,
Till the ghosts were warmer to me
   Than my friends that had grown cold.

I looked and I saw the ghosts
   Dotting plain and mound:
They stood in the blank moonlight,
   But no shadow lay on the ground:

They spoke without a voice
   And they leaped without a sound.

I called: "O my Mother dear,"—
I sobbed: "O my Mother kind,
Make a lonely bed for me
   And shelter it from the wind:

"Tell the others not to come
   To see me night or day:
But I need not tell my friends
   To be sure to keep away."

My Mother raised her eyes,
   They were blank and could not see:
Yet they held me with their stare
   While they seemed to look at me.

She opened her mouth and spoke,·
   I could not hear a word,
While my flesh crept on my bones
   And every hair was stirred.

She knew that I could not hear
   The message that she told
Whether I had long to wait
   Or soon should sleep in the mould:
I saw her toss her shadowless hair
   And wring her hands in the cold.

I strained to catch her words,
   And she strained to make me hear;
But never a sound of words
   Fell on my straining ear.

From midnight to the cockcrow
   I kept my watch in pain
While the subtle ghosts grew subtler
   In the sad night on the wane.

From midnight to the cockcrow
   I watched till all were gone,
Some to sleep in the shifting sea
   And some under turf and stone:
Living had failed and dead had failed,
   And I was indeed alone.

11 *February* 1856.

LET PATIENCE HAVE HER PERFECT WORK

I SAW a bird alone,
   In its nest it sat alone,
For its mate was dead or flown
   Though it was early Spring.
Hard by were buds half-blown,
With cornfields freshly sown:

It could only perch and moan
    That used to sing:
Droop in sorrow left alone:
    A sad sad thing.

I saw a star alone,
In blue heaven it hung alone,
A solitary throne
    In the waste of space:
Where no moon-glories are,
Where not a second star
Beams through night from near or far
    To that lone place.
Its beauties all unknown,
Its glories all alone,
    Sad in heaven's face.

Doth the bird desire a mate,
Pine for a second mate,
Whose first joy was so great
    With its own dove?
Doth the star supreme in night
Desire a second light
To make it seem less bright,
In the shrine of heavenly height
    That is above?—

Ah better wait alone,
In nest or heaven alone,

Forsaken or unknown :
Till, time being past and gone,
Full eternity rolls on,
While patience reaps what it has sown
In the harvest-land of love.

12 *March* 1856.

IN THE LANE

WHEN my love came home to me,
    Pleasant summer bringing,
Every tree was out in leaf,
    Every bird was singing.

There I met her in the lane
    By those waters gleamy,
Met her toward the fall of day,
    Warm and dear and dreamy.
Did I loiter in the lane?
    None was there to see me.

Only roses in the hedge,
    Lilies on the river,
Saw our greeting fast and fond,
    Counted gift and giver,
Saw me take her to my home,
    Take her home for ever.

3 *May* 1856.

ACME

SLEEP, unforgotten sorrow, sleep awhile :
  Make even awhile as though I might forget;
  Let the wound staunch thy tedious fingers
Till once again I look abroad and smile,
Warmed in the sunlight : let no tears defile
  This hour's content, no conscious thorns beset.
  My path : O sorrow, slumber, slumber yet
A moment, rouse not yet the smouldering pile.
So shalt thou wake again with added strength,
  O unforgotten sorrow, stir again
  The slackening fire, refine the lulling pain
  To quickened torture and a subtler edge.
  The wrung cord snaps at last : beneath the wedge
The toughest oak groans long but rends at length.

9 *May* 1856.

A BED OF FORGET-ME-NOTS

IS Love so prone to change and rot
We are fain to rear Forget-me-not
By measure in a garden-plot?—

I love its growth at large and free
By untrod path and unlopped tree,
Or nodding by the unpruned hedge,
Or on the water's dangerous edge
Where flags and meadowsweet blow rank
With rushes on the quaking bank.

Love is not taught in learning's school,
Love is not parcelled out by rule:
Hath curb or call an answer got?—
So free must be Forget-me-not.
Give me the flame no dampness dulls,
The passion of the instinctive pulse,
Love steadfast as a fixed star,
Tender as doves with nestlings are,
More large than time, more strong than death:
  This all creation travails of—
She groans not for a passing breath—
  This is Forget-me-not and Love.

17 *June* 1856.

LOOK ON THIS PICTURE AND ON THIS

I WISH we once were wedded,—then I must be true:
You should hold my will in yours to do or to undo:
But I hate myself now, Eva, when I look at you.

You have seen her hazel eyes, her warm dark skin,
Dark hair—but oh those hazel eyes a devil is dancing in:—
You, my saint, lead up to heaven, she lures down to sin.

She's so redundant, stately:—in truth now have you seen
Ever anywhere such beauty, such a stature, such a mien?
She may be queen of devils, but she's every inch a queen.

If you sing to me, I hear her subtler sweeter still
Whispering in each tender cadence strangely sweet to fill
All that lacks in music, all my soul and sense and will.

But you ask, "Why struggle? I have given you up:
Take again your pledges, snap the cord and break the cup:
Feast you with your temptation, for I in heaven will sup."

Can I bear to think upon you strong to break not bend,
Pale with inner intense passion, silent to the end,
Bear to leave you, bear to grieve you, O my dove, my friend?

Listening so, I hide mine eyes and fancy years to come:
You cherished in another home with no cares burdensome:
You straitened in a winding-sheet, pulseless, at peace, and dumb.

Open house and heart, barred to me alone the door:
Children bound to meet her, babies crow before:
Blessed wife and blessed mother whom I may see no more.

Or I fancy — In the grave her comely body lies:
She is 'tiring for the Bridegroom till the morning star shall rise,
Then to shine a glory in the nuptials of the skies.

No more yearning tenderness, no more pale regret:
  She will not look for me when the marriage-guests
    are set,
  She joys with joy eternal as we had never met.

I would that one of us were dead, were gone no more
    to meet,
Or she and I were dead together stretched here at
    your feet:
That she and I were strained together in one winding-
    sheet.

How have you the heart to face me with that passion
    in your stare
Deathly silent? Weep before me, rave at me in your
    despair: —
If you keep patience, wings will spring and a halo from
    your hair.

  See now how proud you are, like us after all, no
    saint:
Not so upright but that you are bowed with the old
    bent:
White at white-heat, tainted with the devil's special
    taint.

Did I love you? Never from the first cold day to this:
You are not sufficient for my aim of life, my bliss:
You are not sufficient, but I found the one that is.

Then did I never love you ? — ah the sting struck
    home at last !
You are drooping, fainting, dying — the worst of
    death is past —
A light is on your face from the nearing heaven
    forecast.

Never ? — yes I loved you then : I loved, the word
    still charms :
For the first time, last time, lie here in my heart,
    my arms,
For the first last time, as if I shielded you from
    harms.

For after all I loved you, loved you then, I love you
    yet :
Listen, love, I love you : see, the seal of truth is set
  On my face, in tears — you cannot see ? then feel
    them wet.

Pause at heaven's dear gate, look back, one moment
    back to grieve :
You go home through death to life : but I, I still
    must live :
On the threshold of heaven's love, O love, can you
    forgive ? —

Fully, freely, fondly, with heart-truth above an oath,
With eager utter pardon given unasked and nothing
    loth,
Heaping coals of fire upon our heads, forgiving both.

AND ON THIS

One word more — not one! One look more — too late, too late!
Lapped in love she sleeps who was lashed with scorn and hate:
Nestling in the lap of Love the dove has found a mate.

Night has come, the night of rest: day will come, that day:
To her glad dawn of glory kindled from the deathless ray:
To us a searching fire and strict balances to weigh.

The tearless tender eyes are closed, the tender lips are dumb —
I shall not see or hear them more until that day shall come:
Then they must speak; what will they say? — what then will be the sum? —

Shall we stand upon the left, and she upon the right —
We smirched with endless death and shame, she glorified in white —
Will she sound our accusation in intolerable light?

12 *July* 1856.

GONE BEFORE

SHE was most like a rose when it flushes rarest,
  She was most like a lily when it blows fairest,
She was most like a violet sweetest on the bank:
Now she's only like the snow, cold and blank,
  After the sun sank.

She left us in the early days; she would not linger
For orange blossoms in her hair, or ring on finger:
  Did she deem windy grass more good than these?
Now the turf that's between us and the hedging trees
  Might as well be seas.

I had trained a branch she shelters not under,
I had reared a flower she snapped asunder:
  In the bush and on the stately bough
Birds sing; she who watched them track the plough
  Cannot hear them now.

Every bird has a nest hidden somewhere
For itself and its mate and joys that come there,
  Though it soar to the clouds, finding there its rest:
You sang in the height, but no more with eager breast
  Stoop to your own nest.

If I could win you back from heaven-gate lofty,
Perhaps you would but grieve, returning softly:
Surely they would miss you in the blessed throng,
　Miss your sweet voice in their sweetest song,
　　　Reckon time too long.

Earth is not good enough for you, my sweet, my
　　　sweetest;
Life on earth seemed long to you, though to me
　　　fleetest;
I would not wish you back if a wish would do:
　Only, love, I long for heaven with you,
　　　Heart-pierced through and through.

12 *July* 1856.

LIGHT LOVE

"OH sad thy lot before I came,
　　But sadder when I go,—
My presence but a flash of flame,
　A transitory glow
Between two barren wastes like snow.
　What wilt thou do when I am gone?
　　Where wilt thou rest, my dear?
For cold thy bed to rest upon,
　And cold the falling year
Whose withered leaves are lost and sere."

She hushed the baby at her breast:
    She rocked it on her knee:
"And I will rest my lonely rest,
    Warmed with the thought of thee,
Rest lulled to rest by memory."
She hushed the baby with her kiss,
    She hushed it with her breast:
"Is death so sadder much than this?
    Sure death that builds a nest
For those who elsewhere cannot rest."

"Oh sad thy note, my mateless dove,
    With tender nestling cold:
But hast thou ne'er another love
    Left from the days of old
To build thy nest of silk and gold?
To warm thy paleness to a blush
    When I am far away, —
To warm thy coldness to a flush
    And turn thee back to May,
And turn thy twilight back to day."

She did not answer him a word,
    But leaned her face aside,
Sick with the pain of hope deferred
    And sore with wounded pride:
He knew his very soul had lied.
She strained his baby in her arms,
    His baby to her heart:

"Even let it go, the love that harms;
   We two will never part:
Mine own, his own, how dear thou art!"

"Now never teaze me, tender-eyed,
   Sigh-voiced," he said in scorn:
"For nigh at hand there blooms a bride,
   My bride before the morn:
Ripe-blooming she, as thou forlorn.
Ripe-blooming she, my rose, my peach:
   She woos me day and night:
I watch her tremble in my reach:
   She reddens, my delight,
She ripens, reddens, in my sight."

"And is she like a sunlit rose?
   Am I like withered leaves?
Haste where thy spicèd garden blows:
   But in bare autumn eves
Wilt thou have store of harvest-sheaves?
Thou leavest love, true love behind,
   To seek a love as true:
Go seek in haste,— but wilt thou find?
   Change new again for new,
Pluck up, enjoy, yea trample too.

"Alas for her, poor faded rose,
   Alas for her like me,
Cast down and trampled in the snows."—

"Like thee? nay not like thee:
She leans, but from a guarded tree.
Farewell, and dream as long ago
    Before we ever met:
Farewell: my swift-paced horse seems slow."—
    She raised her eyes, not wet
But hard, to Heaven: "Dost Thou forget?"
28 *October* 1856.

WINTER

SWEET blackbird is silenced with chaffinch and thrush,
Only waistcoated robin still chirps in the bush:
Soft sun-loving swallows have mustered in force,
And winged to the spice-teaming southlands their course.

Plump housekeeper dormouse has tucked himself neat,
Just a brown ball in moss with a morsel to eat:
Armed hedgehog has huddled him into the hedge,
While frogs scarce miss freezing deep down in the sedge.

Soft swallows have left us alone in the lurch,
But robin sits whistling to us from his perch:
If I were red robin, I'd pipe you a tune
Would make you despise all the beauties of June.

But, since that cannot be, let us draw round the fire,
Munch chestnuts, tell stories, and stir the blaze higher:
We'll comfort pinched robin with crumbs, little man,
Till he sings us the very best song that he can.

28 *November* 1856.

A TRIAD

THREE sang of love together: one with lips
    Crimson, with cheeks and bosom in a glow,
Flushed to the yellow hair and finger-tips;
    And one there sang who soft and smooth as snow
    Bloomed like a tinted hyacinth at a show;
And one was blue with famine after love,
    Who like a harpstring snapped rang harsh and low
The burden of what those were singing of.
One shamed herself in love; one temperately
    Grew gross in soulless love, a sluggish wife;
One famished died for love. Thus two of three
    Took death for love and won him after strife;
    One droned in sweetness like a fattened bee:
    All on the threshold, yet all short of life.

18 *December* 1856.

IN AN ARTIST'S STUDIO

ONE face looks out from all his canvases,
    One selfsame figure sits or walks or leans :
We found her hidden just behind those screens,
That mirror gave back all her loveliness.
A queen in opal or in ruby dress,
    A nameless girl in freshest summer-greens,
    A saint, an angel — every canvas means
The same one meaning, neither more nor less.
He feeds upon her face by day and night,
    And she with true kind eyes looks back on him,
Fair as the moon and joyful as the light :
    Not wan with waiting, not with sorrow dim ;
Not as she is, but was when hope shone bright ;
    Not as she is, but as she fills his dream.

24 December 1856.

INTROSPECTIVE

I WISH it were over the terrible pain,
Pang after pang again and again:
First the shattering ruining blow,
Then the probing steady and slow.

Did I wince? I did not faint:
My soul broke but was not bent:
Up I stand like a blasted tree
By the shore of the shivering sea.

On my boughs neither leaf nor fruit,
No sap in my uttermost root,
Brooding in an anguish dumb
On the short past and the long to-come.

Dumb I was when the ruin fell,
Dumb I remain and will never tell;
O my soul, I talk with thee,
But not another the sight must see.

I did not start when the torture stung,
I did not faint when the torture wrung:
Let it come tenfold if come it must,
But I will not groan when I bite the dust.

30 *June* 1857.

DAY-DREAMS

GAZING through her chamber window
　　Sits my soul's dear soul :
Looking northward, looking southward,
　　Looking to the goal,
Looking back without control.

I have strewn thy path, beloved,
　　With plumed meadowsweet,
Iris and pale perfumed lilies,
　　Roses most complete :
Wherefore pause on listless feet?

But she sits and never answers,
　　Gazing, gazing still
On swift fountain, shadowed valley,
　　Cedared sunlit hill :
Who can guess or read her will?

Who can guess or read the spirit
　　Shrined within her eyes,
Part a longing, part a languor,
　　Part a mere surprise,
While slow mists do rise and rise?

DAY-DREAMS

Is it love she looks and longs for,
   Is it rest or peace,
Is it slumber self-forgetful
   In its utter ease,
Is it one or all of these?

So she sits and doth not answer
   With her dreaming eyes,
With her languid look delicious
   Almost paradise,
Less than happy, over-wise.

Answer me, O self-forgetful —
   Or of what beside? —
Is it day-dream of a maiden,
   Vision of a bride,
Is it knowledge, love, or pride?

Cold she sits through all my kindling,
   Deaf to all I pray:
I have wasted might and wisdom,
   Wasted night and day:
Deaf she dreams to all I say.

Now if I could guess her secret,
   Were it worth the guess? —
Time is lessening, hope is lessening,
   Love grows less and less:
What care I for no or yes?

I will give her stately burial,
  Though, when she lies dead :
For dear memory of the past time,
  Of her royal head,
Of the much I strove and said.

I will give her stately burial,
  Stately willow-branches bent :
Have her carved in alabaster,
  As she dreamed and leant
While I wondered what she meant.

8 *September* 1857.

A NIGHTMARE

Fragment

I HAVE a friend in ghostland —
  Early found, ah me how early lost ! —
Blood-red seaweeds drip along that coastland
  By the strong sea wrenched and tost.

. . . .

If I wake he hunts me like a nightmare :
  I feel my hair stand up, my body creep :
Without light I see a blasting sight there,
  See a secret I must keep.

12 *September* 1857.

FOR ONE SAKE

ONE passed me like a flash of lightning by,
   To ring clear bells of heaven beyond the stars.
Then said I : Wars and rumours of your wars
Are dull with din of what and where and why :
My heart is where these troubles draw not nigh :
   Let me alone till heaven shall burst its bars,
   Break up its fountains, roll its flashing cars
Earthwards with fire to test and purify.
Let me alone to-night, and one night more
   Of which I shall not count the eventide :
Its morrow will not be as days before :
Let me alone to dream, perhaps to weep :
   To dream of her the imperishable bride,
Dream while I wake and dream on while I sleep.

25 *October* 1857.

FROM METASTASIO

FIRST, last, and dearest,
  My love, mine own,
Thee best beloved,
  Thee love alone,
Once and for ever
  So love I thee.

First as a suppliant
  Love makes his moan,
Then as a monarch
  Sets up his throne:
Once and for ever —
  So love I thee.

Circa 1857.

TO-DAY AND TO-MORROW

I

ALL the world is out in leaf,
  Half the world in flower,
Earth has waited weeks and weeks
  For this special hour:
Faint the rainbow comes and goes
  On a sunny shower.

All the world is making love :
　Bird to bird in bushes,
Beast to beast in glades, and frog
　To frog among the rushes :
Wake, O south wind sweet with spice,
　Wake the rose to blushes.

Life breaks forth to right and left—
　Pipe wild-wood notes cheery.
Nevertheless there are the dead
　Fast asleep and weary—
To-day we live, to-day we love,
　Wake and listen, deary.

2

I wish I were dead, my foe,
My friend, I wish I were dead,
With a stone at my tired feet
And a stone at my tired head.

In the pleasant April days
Half the world will stir and sing,
But half the world will slug and rot
　For all the sap of Spring.

29 *June* 1858.

YET A LITTLE WHILE

THESE days are long before I die:
    To sit alone upon a thorn
Is what the nightingale forlorn
Does night by night continually:
She swells her heart to ecstasy
Until it bursts and she can die.

These days are long that wane and wax:
    Waxeth and wanes the ghostly moon,
    Achill and pale in cordial June:
What is it that she wandering lacks?
She seems as one that aches and aches,
Most sick to wane, most sick to wax.

Of all the sad sights in the world
    The downfall of an Autumn leaf
    Is grievous and suggesteth grief:
Who thought when Spring was fresh unfurled
Of this? when Spring-twigs gleamed impearled
Who thought of frost that nips the world?

There are a hundred subtle stings
    To prick us in our daily walk:
    A young fruit cankered on its stalk,
A strong bird snared for all his wings,
A nest that sang but never sings:
Yea sight and sound and silence stings.

YET A LITTLE WHILE

There is a lack in solitude,
   There is a load in throng of life:
   One with another genders strife,
To be alone yet is not good:
I know but of one neighbourhood
At peace and full — death's solitude.

Sleep soundly, dears, who lulled at last
   Forget the bird and all her pains,
   Forget the moon that waxes, wanes,
The leaf, the sting, the frostful blast:
Forget the troublous years that, past
In strife or ache, did end at last.

We have clear call of daily bells,
   A dimness where the anthems are,
   A chancel vault of sky and star,
A thunder if the organ swells:
Alas our daily life — what else? —
Is not in tune with daily bells.

You have deep pause betwixt the chimes
   Of earth and heaven, a patient pause
   Yet glad with rest by certain laws:
You look and long: while oftentimes
Precursive flush of morning climbs,
And air vibrates with coming chimes.

6 *August* 1858.

FATHER AND LOVER

Father

IF underneath the water
    You comb your golden hair
With a golden comb, my daughter,
    Oh would that I were there !
If underneath the wave
You fill a slimy grave,
Would that I, who could not save,
    Might share.

Lover

If my love Hero queens it
In summer Fairyland,
    What would I be
    But the ring on her hand?
        Her cheek when she leans it
    Would lean on me : —
        Or sweet, bitter-sweet,
    The flower that she wore
        When we parted, to meet
    On the hither shore
    Any more? never more.

Circa 1858.

WHAT GOOD SHALL MY LIFE DO ME?

NO hope in life : yet is there hope
In death, the threshold of man's scope.
Man yearneth (as the heliotrope

For ever seeks the sun) through light,
Through dark, for Love : all, read aright,
Is Love, for Love is infinite.

Shall not this infinite Love suffice
To feed thy dearth?   Lift heart and eyes
Up to the hills, grow glad and wise.

The hills are glad because the sun
Kisses their round tops every one
Where silver fountains laugh and run :

Smooth pebbles shine beneath : beside,
The grass, mere green, grows myriad-eyed
With pomp of blossoms veined or pied.

So every nest is glad whereon
The sun in tender strength has shone :
So every fruit he glows upon :

So every valley depth, whose herds
At pasture praise him without words :
So the winged ecstasies of birds.

If there be any such thing, what
Is there by sunlight betters not?
Nothing except dead things that rot.

Thou then who art not dead, and fit,
Like blasted tree beside the pit,
But for the axe that levels it,

Living show life of Love, whereof
The force wields earth and heaven above :
Who knows not Love begetteth Love?

Love in the gracious rain distils :
Love moves the subtle fountain-rills
To fertilize uplifted hills,

And seedful valleys fertilize :
Love stills the hungry lion's cries,
And the young raven satisfies :

Love hangs this earth in space : Love rolls
Fair worlds rejoicing on their poles,
And girds them round with aureoles :

Love lights the sun : Love through the dark
Lights the moon's evanescent arc :
Same Love lights up the glow-worm's spark :

Love rears the great : Love tends the small :
Breaks off the yoke, breaks down the wall :
Accepteth all, fulfilleth all.

O ye who taste that Love is sweet,
Set waymarks for the doubtful feet
That stumble on in search of it.

Sing hymns of Love, that those who hear
Far off in pain may lend an ear,
Rise up and wonder and draw near.

Lead lives of Love, that others who
Behold your lives may kindle too
With Love and cast their lots with you.

27 *August* 1859.

COUSIN KATE

I WAS a cottage-maiden
  Hardened by sun and air,
Contented with my cottage-mates,
  Not mindful I was fair.
Why did a great lord find me out
  And praise my flaxen hair?
Why did a great lord find me out
  To fill my heart with care?

He lured me to his palace-home —
  Woe's me for joy thereof —
To lead a shameless shameful life,
  His plaything and his love.

He wore me like a golden knot,
    He changed me like a glove:
So now I moan an unclean thing
    Who might have been a dove.

O Lady Kate, my Cousin Kate,
    You grew more fair than I:
He saw you at your father's gate,
    Chose you and cast me by.
He watched your steps along the lane,
    Your sport among the rye:
He lifted you from mean estate
    To sit with him on high.

Because you were so good and pure
    He bound you with his ring:
The neighbours call you good and pure,
    Call me an outcast thing.
Even so I sit and howl in dust,
    You sit in gold and sing:
Now which of us has tenderer heart?
    You had the stronger wing.

O Cousin Kate, my love was true,
    Your love was writ in sand:
If he had fooled not me but you,
    If you stood where I stand,
He had not won me with his love
    Nor bought me with his land:
I would have spit into his face
    And not have taken his hand.

Yet I've a gift you have not got
  And seem not like to get:
For. all your clothes and wedding-ring
  I've little doubt you fret.
My fair-haired son, my shame, my pride,
  Cling closer, closer yet:
Your sire would give broad lands for one
  To wear his coronet.

18 *November* 1859.

SISTER MAUDE

WHO told my mother of my shame,
  Who told my father of my dear?
Oh who but Maude, my sister Maude,
  Who lurked to spy and peer.

Cold he lies, as cold as stone,
  With his clotted curls about his face:
The comeliest corpse in all the world
  And worthy of a queen's embrace.

You might have spared his soul, sister,
  Have spared my soul, your own soul too:
Though I had not been born at all,
  He'd never have looked at you.

K

My father may sleep in Paradise,
  My mother at Heaven-gate :
But sister Maude shall get no sleep·
  Either early or late.

My father may wear a golden gown,
  My mother a crown may win ;
If my dear and I knocked at Heaven-gate
  Perhaps they'd let us in :
But sister Maude, O sister Maude,
  Bide *you* with death and sin.

Circa 1860.

PROMISES LIKE PIE-CRUST

PROMISE me no promises,
  So will I not promise you :
Keep we both our liberties,
  Never false and never true :
Let us hold the die uncast,
  Free to come as free to go :
For I cannot know your past,
  And of mine what can you know?

You, so warm, may once have been
  Warmer towards another one :
I, so cold, may once have seen
  Sunlight, once have felt the sun :

BETTER SO

  ' Who shall show us if it was
    Thus indeed in time of old?
Fades the image from the glass,
    And the fortune is not told.

If you promised, you might grieve
    For lost liberty again:
If I promised, I believe
    I should fret to break the chain:
Let us be the friends we were,
    Nothing more but nothing less:
Many thrive on frugal fare
    Who would perish of excess.

20 *April* 1861.

BETTER SO

FAST asleep, mine own familiar friend,
    Fast asleep at last:
    Though the pain was strong,
    Though the struggle long,
      It is past:
All thy pangs are at an end.

Whilst I weep, whilst death-bells toll,
    Thou art fast asleep,
With idle hands upon thy breast
     And heart at rest:
    Whilst I weep
Angels sing around thy singing soul.

BETTER SO

Who would wish thee back upon the rough
   Wearisome dangerous road?
   Wish back thy toil-spent soul
     Just at the goal?
     My soul, praise God
For one dear soul which hath enough.

I would not fetch thee back to hope with me
   A sickening hope deferred,
   To taste the cup that slips
     From thirsty lips:
     Hast thou not heard
What was to hear, and seen what was to see?

I would not speak the word if I could raise
   My dead to life:
   I would not speak
   If I could flush thy cheek
   And rouse thy pulses' strife
And send thy feet on the once-trodden ways.

   How could I meet the dear rebuke
     If thou shouldst say:
     " O friend of little faith,
     Good was my lot of death,
       And good my day
   Of rest, and good the sleep I took "?

13 December 1861.

OUR WIDOWED QUEEN

THE Husband of the widow care for her,
    The Father of the fatherless :
The faithful Friend, the abiding Comforter,
    Watch over her to bless.

Full twenty years of blameless married faith,
    Of love and honour questioned not,
Joys, griefs imparted : for the first time Death
    Sunders the common lot.

Christ help the desolate Queen upon her throne,
    Strengthen her hands, confirm her heart :
For she henceforth must bear a load alone
    Borne until now in part.

Christ help the desolate Woman in her home,
    Broken of heart, indeed bereft :
Shrinking from solitary days to come,
    Beggared though much is left.

Rise up, O Sons and Daughters of the Dead,
    Weep with your Mother where she weeps :
Yet not as sorrowing without hope be shed
    Your tears : he only sleeps.

Rise up, O Sons and Daughters of the realm,
  In pale reflected sorrow move :
Revere the widowed hand that holds the helm,
  Love her with double love.

In royal patience of her soul possest
  May she fulfil her length of days :
Then may her children rise and call her blest,
  Then may her Husband praise.
16 *December* 1861.

IN PROGRESS

TEN years ago it seemed impossible
  That she should ever grow so calm as this,
With self-remembrance in her warmest kiss
And dim dried eyes like an exhausted well.
Slow-speaking when she has some fact to tell,
  Silent with long-unbroken silences,
  Centred in self yet not unpleased to please,
Gravely monotonous like a passing bell.
Mindful of drudging daily common things,
  Patient at pastime, patient at her work,
    Wearied perhaps but strenuous certainly.
    Sometimes I fancy we may one day see
  Her head shoot forth seven stars from where they lurk
And her eyes lightnings and her shoulders wings.
31 *March* 1862.

SEASONS

OH the cheerful Budding-time !
   When thorn-hedges turn to green,
When new leaves of elm and lime
   Cleave and shed their winter screen;
Tender lambs are born and baa,
   North wind finds no snow to bring,
Vigorous Nature laughs " Ha ha ! "
   In the miracle of Spring.

Oh the gorgeous Blossom-days !
   When broad flag-flowers drink and blow,
In and out in Summer-blaze
   Dragon-flies flash to and fro ;
Ashen branches hang out keys ;
   Oaks put forth the rosy shoot,
Wandering herds wax sleek at ease,
   Lovely blossoms end in fruit.

Oh the shouting Harvest-weeks !
   Mother Earth grown fat with sheaves;
Thrifty gleaner finds who seeks ;
   Russet-golden pomp of leaves
Crowns the woods, to fall at length ;
   Bracing winds are felt to stir,
Ocean gathers up her strength,
   Beasts renew their dwindled fur.

JUNE

Oh the starving Winter lapse !
　Ice-bound, hunger-pinched, and dim ;
Dormant roots recall their saps,
　Empty nests show black and grim.
Short-lived sunshine gives no heat,
　Undue buds are nipped by frost,
Snow sets forth a winding-sheet,
　And all hope of life seems lost.

20 January 1863.

JUNE

COME, cuckoo, come :
　　Come again, swift swallow :
Come and welcome ! when you come
　　Summer's sure to follow :
　　June the month of months
　　Flowers and fruitage brings too,
When green trees spread shadiest boughs,
　　When each wild bird sings too.

　　May is scant and crude,
　　　Generous June is riper :
Birds fall silent in July,
　　　June has its woodland piper :
Rocks upon the maple-tops
　　　Homely-hearted linnet,
Full in hearing of his nest
　　　And the dear ones in it.

If the year would stand
   Still at June for ever,
With no further growth on land
   Nor further flow of river,
If all nights were shortest nights
And longest days were all the seven,
This might be a merrier world
   To my mind to live in.

5 *February* 1862.

JESS AND JILL

JESS and Jill are pretty girls,
   Plump and well to do,
In a cloud of windy curls:
   Yet I know who
Loves me more than curls or pearls.

I'm not pretty, not a bit —
   Thin and sallow-pale;
When I trudge along the street
   I don't need a veil:
Yet I have one fancy hit.

Jess and Jill can trill and sing
   With a flute-like voice,
Dance as light as bird on wing,
   Laugh for careless joys:
Yet it's I who wear the ring.

Jess and Jill will mate some day,
    Surely, surely:
Ripen on to June through May,
While the sun shines make their hay —
    Slacken steps demurely:
Yet even there I lead the way.

20 *February* 1863.

HELEN GREY

BECAUSE one loves you, Helen Grey,
    Is that a reason you should pout,
And like a March wind veer about,
And frown, and say your shrewish say?
Don't strain the cord until it snaps,
    Don't split the sound heart with your wedge,
    Don't cut your fingers with the edge
Of your keen wit; you may perhaps.

Because you're handsome, Helen Grey,
    Is that a reason to be proud?
    Your eyes are bold, your laugh is loud,
Your steps go mincing on their way;
But so you miss that modest charm
    Which is the surest charm of all;
    Take heed, you yet may trip and fall,
And no man care to stretch his arm.

Stoop from your cold height, Helen Grey,
  Come down, and take a lowlier place,
  Come down, to fill it now with grace;
Come down you must perforce some day:
For years cannot be kept at bay,
  And fading years will make you old;
  Then in their turn will men seem cold,
When you yourself are nipped and grey.

23 *February* 1863.

A DUMB FRIEND

I PLANTED a young tree when I was young:
  But now the tree is grown and I am old:
There wintry robin shelters from the cold
    And tunes his silver tongue.

A green and living tree I planted it,
A glossy-foliaged tree of evergreen:
All through the noontide heat it spread a screen
    Whereunder I might sit.

But now I only watch it where it towers:
I, sitting at my window, watch it tost
By rattling gale, or silvered by the frost:
    Or, when sweet summer flowers,

Wagging its round green head with stately grace
In tender winds that kiss it and go by:

It shows a green full age : and what show I ?
    A faded wrinkled face.

So often have I watched it, till mine eyes
Have filled with tears and I have ceased to see,
That now it seems a very friend to me,
    In all my secrets wise.

A faithful pleasant friend, who year by year
Grew with my growth and strengthened with my
    strength,
But whose green lifetime shows a longer length :
    When I shall not sit here

It still will bud in spring, and shed rare leaves
In autumn, and in summer-heat give shade,
And warmth in winter : when my bed is made
    In shade the cypress weaves.

24 *March* 1863.

TO-MORROW

WHERE my heart is (wherever that may be)
    Might I but follow !
If you fly thither over lane and lea
  O honey-seeking bee,
    O careless swallow,
Bid some for whom I watch keep watch for me.

Alas that we must dwell, my heart and I,
   So far asunder!
Hours wax to days, and days and days creep by:
  I watch with wistful eye,
    I wait and wonder:
When will that day draw nigh, that hour draw nigh?

Not yesterday, and not I think to-day:
   Perhaps to-morrow.
Day after day "to-morrow" thus I say:
  I watched so yesterday
    In hope and sorrow;
Again to-day I watch the accustomed way.

25 June 1863.

MARGERY

WHAT shall we do with Margery?
    She lies and cries upon her bed,
  All lily-pale from foot to head;
Her heart is sore as sore can be:
Poor guileless shamefaced Margery.

  A foolish girl, to love a man
    And let him know she loved him so!
She should have tried a different plan:
    Have loved, but not have let him know:
    Then he perhaps had loved her so.

MARGERY

What can we do with Margery
  Who has no relish for her food?
We'd take her with us to the sea —
  Across the sea — but where's the good?
She'd fret alike on land and sea.

Yes, what the neighbours say is true:
  Girls should not make themselves so cheap.
But now it's done what can we do?
  I hear her moaning in her sleep,
  Moaning and sobbing in her sleep.

I think — and I'm of flesh and blood —
  Were I that man for whom she cares,
  I would not cost her tears and prayers
To leave her just alone like mud,
  Fretting her simple heart with cares.

A year ago she was a child,
  Now she's a woman in her grief:
  The year's now at the falling leaf;
At budding of the leaves she smiled:
Poor foolish harmless foolish child.

It was her own fault? so it was.
  If every own fault found us out,
  Dogged us and snared us roundabout,
What comfort should we take because
  Not half our due we thus wrung out?

At any rate the question stands:
   What now to do with Margery,
A weak poor creature on our hands?
   Something we must do: I'll not see
   Her blossom fade, sweet Margery.

Perhaps a change may after all
   Prove best for her: to leave behind
   These home-sights seen time out of mind;
To get beyond the narrow wall
Of home, and learn home is not all.

Perhaps this way she may forget,
   Not all at once, but in a while:
May come to wonder how she set
   Her heart on this slight thing, and smile
   At her own folly, in a while.

Yet this I say and I maintain:
   Were I the man she's fretting for,
   I should my very self abhor
If I could leave her to her pain,
Uncomforted to tears and pain.

1 *October* 1863.

LAST NIGHT

WHERE were you last night? I watched at
the gate;
I went down early, I stayed down late.
   Were you snug at home, I should like to know,
Or were you in the coppice wheedling Kate?

   She's a fine girl, with a fine clear skin;
Easy to woo, perhaps not hard to win.
   Speak up like a man and tell me the truth:
I'm not one to grow downhearted and thin.

   If you love her best, speak up like a man;
It's not I will stand in the light of your plan:
   Some girls might cry and scold you a bit,
And say they couldn't bear it; but I can.

   Love was pleasant enough, and the days went fast;
Pleasant while it lasted, but it needn't last;
   Awhile on the wax, and awhile on the wane,
Now dropped away into the past.

   Was it pleasant to you? to me it was:
Now clean gone as an image from glass,
   As a goodly rainbow that fades away,
As dew that steams upward from the grass,

As the first spring day or the last summer day,
As the sunset flush that leaves heaven grey,
   As a flame burnt out for lack of oil,
Which no pains relight or ever may.

Good luck to Kate and good luck to you :
I guess she'll be kind when you come to woo.
   I wish her a pretty face that will last,
I wish her a husband steady and true.

Hate you? not I, my very good friend;
All things begin and all have an end.
   But let broken be broken; I put no faith
In quacks who set up to patch and mend.

Just my love and one word to Kate —
Not to let time slip if she means to mate;
   For even such a thing has been known
As to miss the chance while we weigh and wait.

November 1863.

IF

IF he would come to-day, to-day, to-day,
   Oh what a day to-day would be!
But now he's away, miles and miles away
   From me across the sea.

O little bird, flying, flying, flying
   To your nest in the warm west,
Tell him as you pass that I am dying,
   As you pass home to your nest.

I have a sister, I have a brother,
   A faithful hound, a tame white dove;
But I had another, once I had another,
   And I miss him, my love, my love!

In this weary world it is so cold, so cold,
   While I sit here all alone;
I would not like to wait and to grow old,
   But just to be dead and gone.

Make me fair when I lie dead on my bed,
   Fair where I am lying:
Perhaps he may come and look upon me dead —
   He for whom I am dying.

Dig my grave for two, with a stone to show it,
   And on the stone write my name:
If he never comes, I shall never know it,
   But sleep on all the same.

12 *April* 1864.

SUNSHINE

"There's little sunshine in my heart,
    Slack to spring, lead to sink :
There's little sunshine in the world,
    I think."

" There's glow of sunshine in my heart
    (Cool wind, cool the glow) :
There's flood of sunshine in the world,
    I know."

Now if of these one spoke the truth,
    One spoke more or less :
But which was which I will not tell :
    You guess.

31 *May* 1864.

MEETING

IF we shall live, we live:
If we shall die, we die:
If we live we shall meet again:
But to-night, good-bye.
One word, let but one be heard —
What, not one word?

If we sleep we shall wake again
And see to-morrow's light:
If we wake, we shall meet again:
But to-night, good-night.
Good-night, my lost and found —
Still not a sound?

If we live, we must part:
If we die, we part in pain:
If we die, we shall part
Only to meet again.
By those tears on either cheek,
To-morrow you will speak.

To meet, worth living for:
Worth dying for, to meet.
To meet, worth parting for:
Bitter forgot in sweet.
To meet, worth parting before,
Never to part more.

11 *June* 1864.

UNDER WILLOWS

UNDER willows among the graves
    One was walking, ah welladay!
Where each willow her green boughs waves,
    Come April prime, come May.
Under willows among the graves
    She met her lost love, ah welladay!
Where in Autumn each wild wind raves
    And whirls sere leaves away.

He looked at her with a smile,
She looked at him with a sigh,
    Both paused to look awhile:
    Then he passed by,—
Passed by and whistled a tune:
She stood silent and still:
It was the sunniest day in June,
    Yet one felt a chill.

Under willows among the graves
I know a certain black black pool
Scarce wrinkled when Autumn raves,
    Under the turf is cool;
Under the water it must be cold:
Winter comes cold when Summer's past:
Though she live to be old, so old,
    She shall die at last.

27 *July* 1864.

A SKETCH

THE blindest buzzard that I know
    Does not wear wings to spread and stir;
Nor does my special mole wear fur,
And grub among the roots below:
    He sports a tail indeed, but then
    It's to a coat: he's man with men:
    His quill is cut to a pen.

In other points our friend's a mole,
    A buzzard, beyond scope of speech.
    He sees not what's within his reach,
Misreads the part, ignores the whole;
    Misreads the part, so reads in vain,
    Ignores the whole though patent plain,—
    Misreads both parts again.

My blindest buzzard that I know,
    My special mole, when will you see?
    Oh no, you must not look at me,
There's nothing hid for me to show.
    I might show facts as plain as day:
    But, since your eyes are blind, you'd say,
    "Where? What?" and turn away.

15 *August* 1864.

IF I HAD WORDS

IF I had words, if I had words
    At least to vent my misery : —
But muter than the speechless herds
    I have no voice wherewith to cry.
I have no strength to lift my hands,
    I have no heart to lift mine eye,
My soul is bound with brazen bands,
    My soul is crushed and like to die.
My thoughts that wander here and there,
    That wander wander listlessly,
Bring nothing back to cheer my care,
    Nothing that I may live thereby.
My heart is broken in my breast,
    My breath is but a broken sigh —
Oh if there be a land of rest
    It is far off, it is not nigh.
If I had wings as hath a dove,
    If I had wings that I might fly,
I yet would seek the land of love
    Where fountains run which run not dry:
Though there be none that road to tell,
    And long that road is verily :
Then if I lived I should do well,
    And if I died I should but die.
If I had wings as hath a dove,
    I would not sift the what and why,

I would make haste to find out Love,
   If not to find at least to try.
I would make haste to Love, my rest —
   To Love, my truth that doth not lie:
Then if I lived it might be best,
   Or if I died I could but die.

3 *September* 1864.

EN ROUTE

1

LIFE flows down to death: we cannot bind
   That current that it should not flee:
Life flows down to death, as rivers find
   The inevitable sea.

2

Wherefore art thou strange, and not my mother?
Thou hast stolen my heart and broken it:
Would that I might call thy sons "My brother,"
   Call thy daughters "Sister sweet":
Lying in thy lap, not in another,
   Dying at thy feet.

Farewell, land of love, Italy,
   Sister-land of Paradise:
With mine own feet I have trodden thee
   Have seen with mine own eyes:

I remember, thou forgettest me,
    I remember thee.

Blessed be the land that warms my heart,
    And the kindly clime that cheers,
And the cordial faces clear from art,
    And the tongue sweet in mine ears:
Take my heart, its truest tenderest part,
    Dear land, take my tears.

3

    Men work and think, but women feel:
    And so (for I'm a woman, I)
    And so I should be glad to die,
And cease from impotence of zeal,
And cease from hope, and cease from dread,
    And cease from yearnings without gain,
    And cease from all this world of pain,
And be at peace among the dead.

Why should I seek and never find
    That something which I have not had?
    Fair and unutterably sad
The world hath sought time out of mind.
Our words have been already said,
    Our deeds have been already done:
    There's nothing new beneath the sun,
But there is peace among the dead.

June 1865.

HUSBAND AND WIFE

"OH kiss me once before I go,
　　To make amends for sorrow :
Oh kiss me once before we part,
　　For we mayn't meet to-morrow.

"And I was wrong to force your will,
　　And wrong to mar your life :
But kiss me once before we part
　　Because you are my wife."

She turned her head and tossed her head,
　　And puckered up her brow :
"I never kissed you yet," said she,
　　"And I'll not kiss you now.

"Though I'm your wife by might and right
　　And forsworn marriage vow,
I never loved you yet," said she,
　　" And I don't love you now."

So he went sailing on the sea,
　　And she sat crossed and dumb,
While he went sailing on the sea
　　Where the storm-winds come.

He'd been away a month and day
  Counting from morn to morn:
And many buds had turned to leaves,
  And many lambs been born,

And many buds had turned to flowers
  For Spring was in a glow,
When she was laid upon her bed
  As white and cold as snow.

"Oh let me kiss my baby once,
  Once before I die:
And bring it sometimes to my grave
  To teach it where I lie.

"And tell my husband, when he comes
  Safe back from sea,
To love the baby that I leave
  If ever he loved me:

"And tell him, not for might or right
  Or forsworn marriage vow,
But for the helpless baby's sake,
  I would have kissed him now."

12 *July* 1865.

WHAT TO DO?

O MY love and my own own deary!
What shall I do? my love is weary.
Sleep, O friend, on soft downy pillow,
Pass, O friend, as wind or as billow,
    And I'll wear the willow.

No stone at his head be set,
A swelling turf be his coverlet,
Bound round with a graveyard wattle,
Hedged round from the trampling cattle
    And the children's prattle.

I myself, instead of a stone,
Will sit by him to dwindle and moan:
Sit and weep with a bitter weeping,
Sit and weep where my love lies sleeping,
    While my life goes creeping.

4 *August* 1865.

IN A CERTAIN PLACE

I FOUND Love in a certain place
  . Asleep and cold — or cold and dead? —
All ivory-white upon his bed,
    All ivory-white his face.

His hands were folded
On his quiet breast,
To his figure laid at rest
Chilly bed was moulded.

His hair hung lax about his brow,
I had not seen his face before:
Or, if I saw it once, it wore
Another aspect now.
No trace of last night's sorrow,
No shadow of to-morrow:
All at peace (thus all sorrows cease),
All at peace.

I wondered: Were his eyes
Soft or falcon-clear?
I wondered: As he lies
Does he feel me near?
In silence my heart spoke
And wondered: If he woke
And found me sitting nigh him
And felt me sitting by him,
If life flushed to his cheek,
He living man with men,
Then if I heard him speak
Oh should I know him then?

6 *March* 1866.

CANNOT SWEETEN

"IF that's water you wash your hands in,
 Why is it black as ink is black?"
"Because my hands are foul with my folly:
 Oh the lost time that comes not back!"

"If that's water you bathe your feet in,
 Why is it red as wine is red?"
"Because my feet sought blood in their goings,
 Red, red is the track they tread."

"Slew you mother or slew you father
 That your foulness passeth not by?"
"Not father, and oh not mother:
 I slew my love with an evil eye."

"Slew you sister or slew you brother
 That in peace you have not a part?"
"Not brother and oh not sister:
 I slew my love with a hardened heart.

"He loved me because he loved me,
 Not for grace or beauty I had:
He loved me because he loved me:
 For his loving me I was glad.

"Yet I loved him not for his loving,
  While I played with his love and truth,
Not loving him for his loving,.
  Wasting his joy, wasting his youth.

"I ate his life as a banquet,
  I drank his life as new wine,
I fattened upon his leanness,
  Mine to flourish and his to pine.

"So his life fled as running water,
  So it perished as water spilt:
If black my hands and my feet as scarlet,
  Blacker, redder my heart of guilt.

"Cold as a stone, as hard, as heavy:
  All my sighs ease it no whit,
All my tears make it no cleaner,
  Dropping, dropping, dropping on it."

8 *March* 1866.

OF MY LIFE

I WEARY of my life
Through the long sultry day,
While happy creatures play
Their harmless lives away : —
　What is my life?

I weary of my life
Through the slow tedious night,
While, earth and heaven's delight,
The moon walks forth in white : —
　What is my life?

If I might, I would die :
My soul should flee away
To-day that is not day
Where sweet souls sing and say —
　If I might die !

If I might, I would die :
My body out of sight,
All night that is not night
My soul should walk in white —
　If I might die !

15 *May* 1866.

WHAT COMES?

OH what comes over the sea,
    Shoals and quicksands past:
And what comes home to me,
Sailing slow, sailing fast?

A wind comes over the sea
    With a moan in its blast:
But nothing comes home to me,
Sailing slow, sailing fast.

Let me be, let me be,
    For my lot is cast:
Land or sea all's one to me,
    And sail it slow or fast.

11 *June* 1866.

LOVE'S NAME

LOVE hath a name of Death:
    He gives a breath
And takes away.
Lo we, beneath his sway,
    Grow like a flower;
    To bloom an hour,
    To droop a day,
    And fade away.

Circa 1869.

BY WAY OF REMEMBRANCE

REMEMBER, if I claim too much of you,
   I claim it of my brother and my friend:
Have patience with me till the hidden end—
Bitter or sweet, in mercy shut from view.
Pay me my due; though I to pay your due
   Am all too poor, and past what will can mend:
   Thus of your bounty you must give and lend,
Still unrepaid by aught I look to do.
Still unrepaid by aught of mine on earth:
   But overpaid, please God, when recompense
Beyond the mystic Jordan and new birth
   Is dealt to virtue as to innocence;
When Angels singing praises in their mirth
   Have borne you in their arms and fetched you hence.

Will you be there? my yearning heart has cried:
   Ah me, my love, my love, shall I be there,
   To sit down in your glory and to share
Your gladness, glowing as a virgin bride?
Or will another dearer, fairer-eyed,
   Sit nigher to you in your jubilee,
   And mindful one of other will you be
Borne higher and higher on joy's ebbless tide?
Yea, if I love I will not grudge you this:

I too shall float upon that heavenly sea
   And sing my joyful praises without ache;
Your overflow of joy shall gladden me,
   My whole heart shall sing praises for your sake,
And find its own fulfilment in your bliss.

In Resurrection is it awfuller
   That rising of the All or of the Each —
   Of all kins, of all nations, of all speech,
Or one by one of him and him and her?
When dust reanimate begins to stir
   Here, there, beyond, beyond, reach beyond reach;
   While every wave disgorges on its beach,
Alive or dead-in-life, some seafarer.
In Resurrection, on the day of days,
   That day of mourning throughout all the earth,
     In Resurrection may we meet again:
     No more with stricken hearts to part in twain;
   As once in sorrow one, now one in mirth,
One in our resurrection-songs of praise.

I love you and you know it — this at least,
   This comfort is mine own in all my pain:
   You know it, and can never doubt again,
And love's mere self is a continual feast:
Not oath of mine nor blessing-word of priest
   Could make my love more certain or more plain.
   Life as a rolling moon doth wax and wane —
O weary moon, still rounding, still decreased!
Life wanes: and when Love folds his wings above

Tired joy, and less we feel his conscious pulse,
    Let us go fall asleep, dear Friend, in peace ; —
    A little while, and age and sorrow cease ;
  A little while, and love reborn annuls
Loss and decay and death — and all is love.

1870.

AN ECHO FROM WILLOW-WOOD

"O ye, all ye that walk in willow-wood."
D. G. Rossetti.

TWO gazed into a pool, he gazed and she,
    Not hand in hand, yet heart in heart, I think,
  Pale and reluctant on the water's brink,
As on the brink of parting which must be.
Each eyed the other's aspect, she and he,
    Each felt one hungering heart leap up and sink,
    Each tasted bitterness which both must drink,
There on the brink of life's dividing sea.
Lilies upon the surface, deep below
    Two wistful faces craving each for each,
    Resolute and reluctant without speech : —
A sudden ripple made the faces flow,
    One moment joined, to vanish out of reach :
    So those hearts joined, and ah were parted so.

Circa 1870.

GOLDEN HOLLY

COMMON Holly bears a berry
   To make Christmas Robins merry:—
Golden Holly bears a rose,
Unfolding at October's close
To cheer an old Friend's eyes and nose.

Circa 1872.

AN ALPHABET

A is the Alphabet, A at its head;
   A is an Antelope, agile to run.
B is the Baker Boy bringing the bread,
   Or black Bear and brown Bear, both begging for bun.

C is a Cornflower come with the corn;
   C is a Cat with a comical look.
D is a dinner which Dahlias adorn;
   D is a Duchess who dines with a Duke.

E is an elegant eloquent Earl;
   E is an Egg whence an Eaglet emerges.
F is a Falcon, with feathers to furl;
   F is a Fountain of full foaming surges.

G is the Gander, the Gosling, the Goose;
  G is a Garnet in girdle of gold.
H is a Heartsease, harmonious of hues;
  H is a huge Hammer, heavy to hold.

I is an Idler who idles on ice;
  I am I — who will say I am not I?
J is a Jacinth, a jewel of price;
  J is a Jay, full of joy in July.

K is a King, or a Kaiser still higher;
  K is a Kitten, or quaint Kangaroo.
L is a Lute or a lovely-toned Lyre;
  L is a Lily all laden with dew.

M is a Meadow where Meadowsweet blows;
  M is a Mountain made dim by a mist.
N is a Nut — in a nutshell it grows —
  Or a Nest full of Nightingales singing — oh list!

O is an Opal, with only one spark;
  O is an Olive, with oil on its skin.
P is a Pony, a pet in a park;
  P is the Point of a Pen or a Pin.

Q is a Quail, quick-chirping at morn;
  Q is a Quince quite ripe and near dropping.
R is a Rose, rosy red on a thorn;
  R is a red-breasted Robin come hopping.

S is a Snow-storm that sweeps o'er the Sea;
  S is the Song that the swift Swallows sing.
T is the Tea-table set out for tea;
  T is a Tiger with terrible spring.

U, the Umbrella, went up in a shower;
  Or Unit is useful with ten to unite.
V is a Violet veined in the flower;
  V is a Viper of venomous bite.

W stands for the water-bred Whale;
  Stands for the wonderful Wax-work so gay.
X, or XX, or XXX is ale,
  Or Policeman X, exercised day after day.

Y is a yellow Yacht, yellow its boat;
  Y is the Yucca, the Yam, or the Yew.
Z is a Zebra, zigzagged his coat,
  Or Zebu, or Zoöphyte, seen at the Zoo.

Circa 1875.

COR MIO

STILL sometimes in my secret heart of hearts
   I say "Cor mio" when I remember you,
And thus I yield us both one tender due
Welding one whole of two divided parts.
Ah Friend, too wise or unwise for such arts,
   Ah noble Friend, silent and strong and true,
   Would you have given me roses for the rue
For which I bartered roses in love's marts?
So late in autumn one forgets the spring,
   Forgets the summer with its opulence,
The callow birds that long have found a wing,
   The swallows that more lately got them hence:
Will anything like spring, will anything
   Like summer, rouse one day the slumbering sense?

Circa 1875.

WHO SHALL SAY?

I TOILED on, but thou
   Wast weary of the way,
And so we parted: now
   Who shall say
Which is happier — I or thou?

I am weary now
On the solitary way:
But art thou rested, thou?
Who shall say
Which of us is calmer now?

Still my heart's love, thou,
In thy secret way,
Art still remembered now:
Who shall say —
Still rememberest thou?

Circa 1875.

LIFE

OH intolerable life which all life long
Abidest haunted by one dread of death —
Is such life life?   When one considereth,
Then black seems almost white, and discord song.
Alas this solitude where swarms a throng!
   Life slowly grows, and dwindles breath by breath —
   Slowly grows on us, and no word it saith,
Its cords made long and all its pillars strong.
Life wanes apace — a life that but deceives,
   And works and reigns like life, and yet is dead:
Where is the life that dies not but that lives?
The sweet long life immortal, ever young,
The life that wooes us with a silver tongue,
   Whither?   Much said, and much more left unsaid.

Circa 1875.

MEETING

I SAID good-bye in hope;
   But, now we meet again,
I have no hope at all
Of anything but pain,—
Our parting and our meeting
   Alike in vain.

Hope on through all your life
   Until the end, dear friend:
Live through your noble life
   Where joy and promise blend—
I too will live my life
   Until the end.

Long may your vine entwine,
Long may your fig-tree spread,
   Their paradise of shade
Above your cherished head:
My shelter was a gourd,
   And it is dead.

Yet, when out of a grave
We are gathered home at last,
   Then may we own life spilt
No good worth holding fast:—
Death had its bitterness,
   But it is past.

Circa 1875.

LINES

WHERE are the songs I used to sing,
  Where are the notes I used to know?
I have forgotten everything
  I used to know so long ago.
Summer has followed after Spring;
  Now Autumn is so shrunk and sere
I scarcely think a sadder thing
  Can be the Winter of my year.

Circa 1875.

HADRIAN'S DEATH-SONG TRANSLATED

SOUL rudderless, unbraced,
  The body's friend and guest,
  Whither away to-day?
Unsuppled, pale, discased,
  Dumb to thy wonted jest.

1876.

VALENTINES TO MY MOTHER

1876

FAIRER than younger beauties, more beloved
  Than many a wife,
By stress of Time's vicissitudes unmoved
  From settled calm of life;

Endearing rectitude to those who watch
  The verdict of your face,
Raising and making gracious those who catch
  A semblance of your grace:

With kindly lips of welcome, and with pleased
  Propitious eyes benign,
Accept a kiss of homage from your least
  Last Valentine.

1877

OWN Mother dear,
    We all rejoicing here
Wait for each other,
Daughter for Mother,
Sister for Brother,
Till each dear face appear
Transfigured by Love's flame
Yet still the same, —

VALENTINES TO MY MOTHER

The same yet new,—
My face to you,
Your face to me,
Made lovelier by Love's flame
But still the same;
Most dear to see
In halo of Love's flame,
Because the same.

1878

BLESSED Dear and Heart's Delight,
Companion, Friend, and Mother mine,
Round whom my fears and love entwine, —
With whom I hope to stand and sing
Where Angels form the outer ring
Round singing Saints who, clad in white,
Know no more of day or night
Or death or any changeful thing,
Or anything that is not love,
Human love and Love Divine,—
Bid me to that tryst above,
Bless your Valentine.

1879

MOTHER mine,
    Whom every year
Doth endear, —
Before sweet Spring
(That sweetest thing
Brimfull of bliss)
   Sets all the throng
     Of birds a-wooing,
     Billing and cooing, –
Your Valentine
   Sings you a song,
   Gives you a kiss.

1880

MORE shower than shine
    Brings sweet St. Valentine;
Warm shine, warm shower,
Bring up sweet flower on flower.
  Through shower and shine
Loves you your Valentine,
  Through shine, through shower,
Through summer's flush, through autumn's fading
    hour.

1881

TOO cold almost for hope of Spring
    Or firstfruits from the realm of flowers,
Your dauntless Valentine, I bring
    One sprig of love, and sing
    "Love has no Winter hours."

If even in this world love is love
    (This wintry world which felt the Fall),
What must it be in heaven above
    Where love to great and small
    Is all in all?

1882

MY blessed Mother dozing in her chair
    On Christmas Day seemed an embodied Love,
A comfortable Love with soft brown hair
    Softened and silvered to a tint of dove;
A better sort of Venus with an air
    Angelical from thoughts that dwell above;
A wiser Pallas in whose body fair
    Enshrined a blessed soul looks out thereof.
Winter brought holly then; now Spring has brought
    Paler and frailer snowdrops shivering;
And I have brought a simple humble thought —
    I her devoted duteous Valentine —
A lifelong thought which thrills this song I sing,
    A lifelong love to this dear Saint of mine.

1883

A WORLD of change and loss, a world of death,
Of heart and eyes that fail, of labouring breath,
Of pains to bear and painful deeds to do: —
Nevertheless a world of life to come
And love; where you're at home, while in our home
Your Valentine rejoices, having you.

1884

ANOTHER year of joy and grief,
 Another year of hope and fear:
O Mother, is life long or brief?
 We hasten while we linger here.

But, since we linger, love me still
 And bless me still, O Mother mine,
While hand in hand we scale life's hill,
 You guide, and I your Valentine.

1885

ALL the Robin Redbreasts
 Have lived the winter through,
Jenny Wrens have pecked their fill
 And found a work to do;

Families of Sparrows
  Have weathered wind and storm
With Rabbit on the stony hill
  And Hare upon her form.

You and I, my Mother,
  Have lived the winter through,
And still we play our daily parts
  And still find work to do:
And still the cornfields flourish,
  The olive and the vine,
And still you reign my Queen of Hearts
  And I'm your Valentine.

1886

WINTER'S latest snowflake is the snowdrop flower,
  Yellow crocus kindles the first flame of the Spring,
At that time appointed, at that day and hour,
  When life reawakens and hope in everything.

Such a tender snowflake in the wintry weather,
  Such a feeble flamelet for chilled St. Valentine, —
But blest be any weather which finds us still together,
  My pleasure and my treasure, O blessed Mother mine.

MY MOUSE

A VENUS seems my Mouse
 Come safe ashore from foaming seas,
Which in a small way and at ease
 Keeps house.

An Iris seems my Mouse,
Bright bow of that exhausted shower
Which made a world of sweet herbs flower
 And boughs.

A darling Mouse it is: —
Part hope not likely to take wing,
Part memory, part anything
 You please.

Venus-cum-Iris Mouse,
From shifting tides set safe apart,
In no mere bottle, in my heart
 Keep house.

New Year 1877.

A POOR OLD DOG

PITY the sorrows of a poor old dog
  Who wags his tail a-begging in his need;
Despise not even the sorrows of a frog,
  God's creature too, and that's enough to plead;
Spare puss who trusts us dozing on our hearth;
  Spare bunny, once so frisky and so free;
Spare all the harmless creatures of the earth:
  Spare, and be spared — or who shall plead for thee?

Circa 1879.

PARTED

HAD Fortune parted us,
  Fortune is blind;
Had Anger parted us,
  Anger unkind —
But since God parts us
  Let us part humbly,
Bearing our burden
  Bravely and dumbly.

And since there is but one
  Heaven, not another,
Let us not close that door
  Against each other.

God's Love is higher than mine,
   Christ's tenfold proved,
Yet even I would die
   For thee, Beloved.

Circa 1880.

TO-DAY'S BURDEN

"ARISE, depart, for this is not your rest."—
   Oh burden of all burdens, still to arise
And still depart nor rest in any wise!
Rolling, still rolling thus from East to West,
Earth journeys on her immemorial quest,
   Whom a moon chases in no different guise.
   Thus stars pursue their courses, and thus flies
The sun, and thus all creatures manifest
Unrest the common heritage, the ban
   Flung broadcast to all humankind, on all
      Who live — for, living, all are bound to die.
That which is old, we know that it is man.
   These have no rest who sit and dream and sigh,
      Nor have those rest who wrestle and who fall.

Circa 1881.

COUNTERBLAST ON PENNY TRUMPET

IF Mr. Bright retiring does not please,
And Mr. Gladstone staying gives offence,
What can man do which is not one of these?
    Use your own common sense.
Yet he's a brave man who abjures his cause
    For conscience' sake: let byegones be byegones:
Not *this* among the makers of our laws
    The least and last of Johns.

If all our byegones could be piled on shelves
    High out of reach of penny-line Tyrtæus!
If only all of us could see ourselves
    As others see us!

21 *July* 1882.

MICHAEL F. M. ROSSETTI

Born 22 April 1881; Died 24 January 1883.

1

A HOLY Innocent gone home
    Without so much as one sharp wounding word;
A blessed Michael in heaven's lofty dome
    Without a sword.

2

Brief dawn and noon and setting time!
    Our rapid-rounding moon has fled;

A black eclipse before the prime
   Has swallowed up that shining head.
Eternity holds up her looking-glass: —
   The eclipse of Time will pass,
And all that lovely light return to sight.

3

I watch the showers and think of flowers:
   Alas my flower that shows no fruit!
   My snowdrop plucked, my daisy shoot
     Plucked from the root.
Soon Spring will shower, the world will flower,
   A world of buds will promise fruit,
   Pear-trees will shoot and apples shoot
     Sound at the root.
Bud of an hour, far off you flower;
   My bud, far off you ripen fruit;
   My prettiest bud, my straightest shoot,
     Sweet at the root.

4

The youngest bud of five,
The least lamb of the fold,
Bud not to blossom, yet to thrive
   Away from cold:
Lamb which we shall not see
Leap at its pretty pranks,
Our lamb at rest and full of glee
   On heavenly banks.

January 1883.

THE WAY OF THE WORLD

A BOAT that sails upon the sea,
　　Sails far and far and far away:
Who sail in her sing songs of glee,
　　Or watch and pray.

A boat that drifts upon the sea,
　　Silent and void to sun and air:
Who sailed in her have ended glee
　　And watch and prayer.

Circa 1890.

TO MY FIOR-DI-LISA

THE Rose is Love's own flower, and Love's no less
　　The Lily's tenderness.
Then half their dignity must Roses yield
　　To Lilies of the field?
Nay, diverse notes make up true harmony,
　　All-fashioned loves agree:
Love wears the Lily's whiteness, and Love glows
　　In the deep-hearted Rose.

1892.

SLEEPING AT LAST

SLEEPING at last, the trouble and tumult over,
   Sleeping at last, the struggle and horror past,
Cold and white, out of sight of friend and of lover,
   Sleeping at last.

No more a tired heart downcast or overcast,
No more pangs that wring or shifting fears that hover,
   Sleeping at last in a dreamless sleep locked fast.

Fast asleep. Singing birds in their leafy cover
   Cannot wake her, nor shake her the gusty blast.
Under the purple thyme and the purple clover
   Sleeping at last.

Circa 1893.

DEVOTIONAL POEMS

I DO SET MY BOW IN THE CLOUD

THE roses bloom too late for me:
The violets I shall not see:
Even the snowdrops will not come
Till I have passed from home to home:
From home on earth to home in heaven,
Here penitent and there forgiven.

Mourn not, my Father, that I seek
One who is strong when I am weak.
Through the dark passage, verily,
His rod and staff shall comfort me:
He shall support me in the strife
Of death that dieth into life:
He shall support me, He receive
My soul when I begin to live,
And more than I can ask for give.

He from the heaven-gates built above
Hath looked on me in perfect love.
From the heaven-walls to me He calls
To come and dwell within those walls:

With Cherubim and Seraphim
And Angels: yea, beholding Him.

His care for me is more than mine,
Father; His love is more than thine.
Sickness and death I have from thee,
From Him have immortality.
He giveth gladness where He will,
Yet chasteneth His beloved still.

Then tell me: is it not enough
To feel that, when the path is rough
And the sky dark and the rain cold,
His promise standeth as of old?
When heaven and earth have past away
Only His righteous word shall stay,
And we shall know His will is best.
Behold: He is a haven-rest,
A sheltering rock, a hiding-place,
For runners steadfast in the race;
Who, toiling for a little space,
Had light through faith when sight grew dim,
And offered all their world to Him.

December 1847.

DEATH IS SWALLOWED UP IN VICTORY

"TELL me: doth it not grieve thee to lie here,
   And see the cornfields waving not for thee,
Just in the waking summer of the year?"
"I fade from earth, and lo along with me
The season that I love will fade away:
   How should I look for autumn longingly?"
"Yet autumn beareth fruit whilst day by day
   The leaves grow browner with a mellow hue,
Declining to a beautiful decay."
"Decay is death, with which I have to do,
And see it near: behold, it is more good
   Than length of days and length of sorrow too."
"But thy heart hath not dwelt in solitude;
   Many have loved and love thee: dost not heed
Free love, for which in vain have others sued?"
"I thirst for love, love is mine only need,
Love such as none hath borne me nor can bear,
   True love that prompteth thought and word and deed."
"Here it is not: why seek it otherwhere?
   Nay, bow thy head, and own that on this earth
Are many goodly things and sweet and fair."
"There are tears in man's laughter: in his mirth
There is a fearful forward look; and lo
   An infant's cry gives token of its birth."

DEATH IS SWALLOWED UP

"I mark the ocean of Time ebb and flow:
  He who hath care one day and is perplext
To-morrow may have joy in place of woe."
"Evil becomes good: and to this annext
Good becomes evil: speak of it no more:
  My heart is wearied and my spirit vext."
"Is there no place it grieves thee to give o'er?
  Is there no home thou lov'st, and so wouldst fain
Tarry a little longer at the door?"
"I must go hence and not return again:
But the friends whom I have shall come to me,
  And dwell together with me safe from pain."
"Where is that mansion mortals cannot see?
  Behold, the tombs are full of worms: shalt thou
Rise thence and soar up skywards gloriously?"
"Even as the planets shine we know not how,
We shall be raised then, changed yet still the same —
  Being made like Christ, yea being as He is now."
"Thither thou go'st whence no man ever came:
  Death's voyagers return not, and in death
There is no room for speech or sign or fame."
"There is room for repose that comforteth;
There weariness is not: and there content
  Broodeth for ever, and hope hovereth."
"When the stars fall and when the graves are rent,
  Shalt thou have safety? shalt thou look for life
When the great light of the broad sun is spent?"
"These elements shall consummate their strife,
This heaven and earth shall shrivel like a scroll,
  And then be re-created, beauty-rife."

"Who shall abide it when from pole to pole
  The world's foundations shall be overthrown?
Who shall abide to scan the perfect whole?"
  "He who hath strength given to him, not his own:
He who hath faith in that which is not seen,
  And patient hope: who trusts in Love alone."
"Yet thou — the death-struggle must intervene
  Ere thou win rest: think better of it: think
Of all that is and shall be and hath been."
  "The cup my Father giveth me to drink,
Shall I not take it meekly? though my heart
  Tremble a moment, it shall never shrink."
"Satan will wrestle with thee when thou art
  In the last agony; and Death will bring
Sins to remembrance ere thy spirit part."
  "In that great hour of unknown suffering
God shall be with me, and His arm made bare
  Shall fight for me: yea, underneath His wing,
I shall lie safe at rest and freed from care."

20 *February* 1848.

A CHRISTMAS CAROL

THANK God, thank God, we do believe:
Thank God that this is Christmas Eve.
Even as we kneel upon this day,
Even so, the ancient legends say,
Nearly two thousand years ago
The stalled ox knelt, and even so
The ass knelt full of praise, which they
Could not express, while we can pray.
Thank God, thank God, for Christ was born
Ages ago, as on this morn.
In the snow-season undefiled
God came to earth a little child:
He put His ancient glory by
To live for us and then to die.

How shall we thank God? How shall we
Thank Him and praise Him worthily?
What will He have who loved us thus?
What presents will He take from us?
Will He take gold, or precious heap
Of gems? or shall we rather steep
The air with incense, or bring myrrh?
What man will be our messenger
To go to Him and ask His will?
Which having learned, we will fulfil
Though He choose all we most prefer: —
What man will be our messenger?

Thank God, thank God, the Man is found,
Sure-footed, knowing well the ground.
He knows the road, for this the way
He travelled once, as on this day.
He is our Messenger beside,
He is our door and path and Guide:
He also is our Offering:
He is the gift that we must bring.
Let us kneel down with one accord
And render thanks unto the Lord:
For unto us a Child is born
Upon this happy Christmas morn;
For unto us a Son is given,
Firstborn of God and Heir of Heaven.

7 *March* 1849.

FOR ADVENT

SWEET sweet sound of distant waters, falling
   On a parched and thirsty plain:
Sweet sweet song of soaring skylark, calling
   On the sun to shine again:
Perfume of the rose, only the fresher
   For past fertilizing rain:
Pearls amid the sea, a hidden treasure
   For some daring hand to gain: —
Better, dearer than all these
Is the earth beneath the trees:

Of a much more priceless worth
Is the old brown common earth.

Little snow-white lamb, piteously bleating
   For thy mother far away:
Saddest sweetest nightingale, retreating
   With thy sorrow from the day:
Weary fawn whom night has overtaken,
   From the herd gone quite astray:
Dove whose nest was rifled and forsaken
   In the budding month of May: —
Roost upon the leafy trees,
Lie on earth and take your ease:
Death is better far than birth:
You shall turn again to earth.

Listen to the never-pausing murmur
   Of the waves that fret the shore:
See the ancient pine that stands the firmer
   For the storm-shock that it bore:
And the moon her silver chalice filling
   With light from the great sun's store:
And the stars which deck our temple's ceiling
   As the flowers deck its floor:
Look and hearken while you may,
For these things shall pass away:
All these things shall fail and cease:
Let us wait the end in peace.

Let us wait the end in peace, for truly
   That shall cease which was before:

TWO PURSUITS

Let us see our lamps are lighted, duly
  Fed with oil nor wanting more:
Let us pray while yet the Lord will hear us,
  For the time is almost o'er:
Yea, the end of all is very near us:
  Yea, the Judge is at the door.
  Let us pray now, while we may:
  It will be too late to pray
  When the quick and dead shall all
  Rise at the last trumpet-call.

12 *March* 1849.

TWO PURSUITS

A VOICE said "Follow, follow": and I rose
  And followed far into the dreamy night,
Turning my back upon the pleasant light.
It led me where the bluest water flows,
And would not let me drink: where the corn grows
  I dared not pause, but went uncheered by sight
  Or touch: until at length in evil plight
It left me, wearied out with many woes.
Some time I sat as one bereft of sense:
  But soon another voice from very far
    Called, "Follow, follow": and I rose again.
Now on my night has dawned a blessed star:
    Kind steady hands my sinking steps sustain,
And will not leave me till I shall go hence.

12 *April* 1849.

THE WATCHERS

SHE fell asleep among the flowers
In the sober autumn hours.

Three there are about her bed,
At her side and feet and head.

At her head standeth the Cross
For which all else she counted loss:

Still and steadfast at her feet
Doth her Guardian Angel sit:

Prayers of truest love abide
Wrapping her on every side.

The holy Cross standeth alone,
Beneath the white moon, whitest stone.

Evil spirits come not near
Its shadow, shielding from all fear:

Once she bore it in her breast,
Now it certifies her rest.

Humble violets grow around
Its base, sweetening the grassy ground,

Leaf-hidden: so she hid from praise
Of men her pious holy ways.

THE WATCHERS

Higher about it, twining close,
Clingeth a crimson thorny rose:

So from her heart's good seed of love
Thorns sprang below, flowers spring above.

Though yet his vigil doth not cease,
Her Angel sits in perfect peace,

With white folded wings: for she
He watches now is pure as he.

He watches with his loving eyes
For the day when she shall rise:

When full of glory and of grace
She shall behold him face to face.

Though she is safe for ever, yet
Human love doth not forget:

But prays that in her deep
Grave she may sleep a blessed sleep,

Till when time and the world are past
She may find mercy at the last.

So these three do hedge her in
From sorrow, as death does from sin.

So freed from earthly taint and pain
May they all meet in heaven.   Amen.

25 *May* 1850.

BEHOLD, I STAND AT THE DOOR AND KNOCK

WHO standeth at the gate? — A woman old,
    A widow from the husband of her love.
"Oh lady, stay, this wind is piercing cold,
    Oh look at the keen frosty moon above;
I have no home, am hungry, feeble, poor." —
    "I'm really very sorry, but I can
    Do nothing for you; there's the clergyman,"
The lady said, and shivering closed the door.

Who standeth at the gate? — Wayworn and pale
    A grey-haired man asks charity again.
"Kind lady, I have journeyed far, and fail
    Through weariness; for I have begged in vain
Some shelter, and can find no lodging-place."
    She answered: "There's the workhouse very near;
    Go, for they'll certainly receive you there" —
Then shut the door against his pleading face.

Who standeth at the gate? — A stunted child,
    Her sunk eyes sharpened with precocious care.
"Oh lady, save me from a home defiled,
    From shameful sights and sounds that taint the air:
Take pity on me, teach me something good." —
    "For shame, why don't you work instead of cry?
    I keep no young impostors here, not I."
She slammed the door, indignant where she stood.

Who standeth at the gate, and will be heard?
   Arise, O woman, from thy comforts now:
Go forth again to speak the careless word,
   The cruel word unjust, with hardened brow.
But who is this, that standeth not to pray
   As once, but terrible to judge thy sin?
   This whom thou wouldst not succour nor take in
Nor teach but leave to perish by the way.

"Thou didst it not unto the least of these,
   And in them hast not done it unto Me.
Thou wast as a princess rich and at ease —
Now sit in dust and howl for poverty.
Three times I stood beseeching at thy gate,
   Three times I came to bless thy soul and save:
   But now I come to judge for what I gave,
And now at length thy sorrow is too late."

   1 *December* 1851.

ADVENT

"COME," Thou dost say to Angels,
   To blessed Spirits, "Come":
"Come," to the lambs of Thine own flock,
   Thy little ones, "Come home."

"Come," from the many-mansioned house
   The gracious word is sent,
"Come," from the ivory palaces
   Unto the Penitent.

O Lord, restore us deaf and blind,
   Unclose our lips though dumb:
Then say to us, "I come with speed,"
   And we will answer, "Come."

12 *December* 1851.

ALL SAINTS

THEY have brought gold and spices to my King,
   Incense and precious stuffs and ivory:
O holy Mother mine, what can I bring
   That so my Lord may deign to look on me?
They sing a sweeter song than I can sing,
   All crowned and glorified exceedingly:
I, bound on earth, weep for my trespassing, —
   They sing the song of love in heaven, set free.
Then answered me my Mother, and her voice
   Spake to my heart, yea answered in my heart:
"Sing, saith He to the heavens, to earth rejoice:
   Thou also lift thy heart to Him above:
He seeks not thine, but thee such as thou art,
   For lo His banner over thee is Love."

20 *January* 1852.

EYE HATH NOT SEEN

OUR feet shall tread upon the stars
    Less bright than we.
The everlasting shore shall bound
    A fairer sea
    Than that which cold
Now glitters in the sun like gold.

Oh good, oh blest! but who shall say
    How fair, how fair,
Is the light-region where no cloud
    Darkens the air,
    Where weary eyes
Rest on the green of Paradise?

There cometh not the wind nor rain
    Nor sun nor snow:
The Trees of Knowledge and of Life
    Bud there and blow,
    Their leaves and fruit
Fed from an undecaying root.

There Angels flying to and fro
    Are not more white
Than Penitents some while ago,
    Now Saints in light:
    Once soiled and sad —
Cleansed now and crowned, fulfilled and glad.

Now yearning through the perfect rest
    Perhaps they gaze
Earthwards upon their best-beloved
    In all earth's ways:
    Longing, but not
With pain, as used to be their lot.

The hush of that beatitude
    Is ages long,
Sufficing Virgins, Prophets, Saints,
    Till the new song
    Shall be sent up
From lips which drained the bitter cup.

If but the thought of Paradise
    Gives joy on earth,
What shall it be to enter there
    Through second birth?
    To find once more
Our dearest treasure gone before?

To find the Shepherd of the sheep,
    The Lamb once slain,
Who leads His own by living streams —
    Never again
    To thirst, or need
Aught in green pastures where they feed.

But from the altar comes a cry
    Awful and strong

From martyred Saints: "How long," they say,
   "O Lord, how long,
   Holy and True,
Shall vengeance for our blood be due?"

Then the Lord gives them robes of white,
   And bids them stay
In patience till the time be full
   For the last day —
   The day of dread
When the last sentence shall be said;

When heaven and earth shall flee away,
   And the great deep
Shall render up her dead, and earth
   Her sons that sleep,
   And day of grace
Be hid for ever from Thy face.

Oh hide us till Thy wrath be past,
   Our grief, our shame,
With Peter and with Magdalene
   And him whose name
   No record tells
Who by Thy promise with Thee dwells.

1 *May* 1852.

ST. ELIZABETH OF HUNGARY

WHEN if ever life is sweet,
    Save in heart in all a child,
A fair virgin undefiled,
    Knelt she at her Saviour's feet:
While she laid her royal crown,
    Thinking it too mean a thing
    For a solemn offering,
Careless on the cushions down.

Fair she was as any rose,
    But more pale than lilies white:
Her eyes full of deep repose
    Seemed to see beyond our sight.
Hush, she is a holy thing:
    Hush, her soul is in her eyes,
    Seeking far in Paradise
For her Light, her Love, her King.

16 June 1852.

MOONSHINE

FAIR the sun riseth,
    Bright as bright can be,
Fair the sun shineth
    On a fair fair sea.

"Across the water
Wilt thou come with me,
Miles and long miles, love,
Over the salt sea?"

"If thou wilt hold me
Truly by the hand,
I will go with thee
Over sea and sand.

"If thou wilt hold me
That I shall not fall,
I will go with thee,
Love, in spite of all."

Fair the moon riseth
On her heavenly way,
  Making the waters
Fairer than by day.

  A little vessel
Rocks upon the sea,
  Where stands a maiden
Fair as fair can be.

  Her smile rejoices
Though her mouth is mute:
  She treads the vessel
With her little foot.

Truly he holds her
Faithful to his pledge,
  Guiding the vessel
From the water's edge.

Fair the moon saileth
  With her pale fair light,
Fair the girl gazeth
  Out into the night.

Saith she, "Like silver
Shines thy hair, not gold":
  Saith she, "I shiver
In thy steady hold.

"Love," she saith weeping,
"Loose thy hold awhile;
  My heart is freezing
In thy freezing smile."

The moon is hidden
By a silver cloud,
  Fair as a halo
Or a maiden's shroud.

No more beseeching,
Ever on they go:
  The vessel rocketh
Softly to and fro:

And still he holds her
That she shall not fall,
　Till pale mists whiten
Dimly over all.

　Onward and onward,
Far across the sea:
　Onward and onward,
Pale as pale can be:

　Onward and onward,
Ever hand in hand,
　From sun and moonlight
To another land.

16 *June* 1852.

I LOOK FOR THE LORD

OUR wealth has wasted all away,
　Our pleasures have found wings;
The night is long until the day;
　Lord, give us better things —
A ray of light in thirsty night
　And secret water-springs.

Our love is dead, or sleeps, or else
　Is hidden from our eyes:

Our silent love, while no man tells
   Or if it lives or dies.
Oh give us love, O Lord, above
   In changeless Paradise.

Our house is left us desolate,
   Even as Thy word hath said.
Before our face the way is great;
   Around us are the dead.
Oh guide us, save us from the grave,
   As Thou Thy saints hast led.

Lead us where pleasures evermore
   And wealth indeed are placed,
And home on an eternal shore,
   And love that cannot waste:
Where joy Thou art unto the heart,
   And sweetness to the taste.

28 *September* 1852.

THE HEART KNOWETH ITS OWN BITTERNESS

WEEP yet awhile, —
   Weep till that day shall dawn when thou shalt smile:
Watch till the day
When all save only love shall pass away.

Weep, sick and lonely,
Bow thy heart to tears,
For none shall guess the secret
Of thy griefs and fears.
Weep, till the day dawn,
   Refreshing dew:
   Weep till the spring:
   For genial showers
   Bring up the flowers,
   And thou shalt sing
In summertime of blossoming.

Heart-sick and silent,
Weep and watch in pain.
   Weep for hope perished,
Not to live again:
Weep for love's hope and fear
   And passion vain.
   Watch till the day
When all save only love shall pass away.

   Then love rejoicing
Shall forget to weep :
Shall hope or fear no more,
   Or watch, or sleep,
But only love and cease not,
   Deep beyond deep.
Now we sow love in tears,
   But then shall reap.

Have patience as the Lord's own flock of sheep:
Have patience with His love
Who died below, who lives for thee above.

23 *December* 1852.

WHITSUN EVE

THE white dove cooeth in her downy nest,
   Keeping her young ones warm beneath her
      breast:
The white moon saileth through the cool clear sky,
Screened by a tender mist in passing by:
The white rose buds, with thorns upon its stem,
All the more precious and more dear for them:
The stream shines silver in the tufted grass,
The white clouds scarcely dim it as they pass;
Deep in the valleys lily cups are white,
They send up incense all the holy night:
Our souls are white, made clean in Blood once shed:
White blessed Angels watch around our bed: —
O spotless Lamb of God, still keep us so,
Thou who wert born for us in time of snow.

18 *May* 1853.

THERE REMAINETH THEREFORE A REST FOR THE PEOPLE OF GOD

I

Ye have forgotten the exhortation

COME, blessed sleep, most full, most perfect, come:
　　Come, sleep, if so I may forget the whole;
　Forget my body and forget my soul,
Forget how long life is and troublesome.
Come, happy sleep, to soothe my heart or numb,
　　Arrest my weary spirit or control:
　Till light be dark to me from pole to pole,
And winds and echoes and low songs be dumb.
Come, sleep, and lap me into perfect calm,
　　Lap me from all the world and weariness:
Come, secret sleep, with thine unuttered psalm,
　　Safe sheltering in a hidden cool recess:
　Come, heavy dreamless sleep, and close and press
Upon mine eyes thy fingers dropping balm.

II

Which speaketh unto you as unto children

ART thou so weary then, poor thirsty soul?
　　Have patience, in due season thou shalt sleep.
　Mount yet a little while, the path is steep:

Strain yet a little while to reach the goal:
Do battle with thyself, achieve, control:
 Till night come down with blessed slumber deep
 As love, and seal thine eyes no more to weep
Through long tired vigils while the planets roll.
Have patience, for thou too shalt sleep at length,
 Lapt in the pleasant shade of Paradise.
 My Hands that bled for thee shall close thine eyes,
 My Heart that bled for thee shall be thy rest:
I will sustain with everlasting strength,
 And thou, with John, shalt lie upon My breast.

12 *July* 1853.

A HARVEST

O GATE of death, of the blessed night,
 That shall open not again
 On this world of shame and sorrow,
 Where slow ages wax and wane,
Where are signs and seasons, days and nights,
 And mighty winds and rain.

Is the day wearing toward the west?—
 Far off cool shadows pass,
 A visible refreshment
 Across the sultry grass:
Far off low mists are mustering,
 A broken shifting mass.

A HARVEST

Still in the deepest knowledge
Some depth is left unknown:
Still in the merriest music lurks
A plaintive undertone:
Still with the closest friend some throb
Of life is felt alone.

Time's summer breath is sweet, his sands
Ebb sparkling as they flow,
Yet some are sick that this should end
Which is from long ago:—
Are not the fields already white
To harvest in the glow?—

There shall come another harvest
Than was in days of yore:
The reapers shall be Angels,
Our God shall purge the floor:—
No more seed-time, no more harvest,
Then for evermore.

1 *August* 1853.

THE ELEVENTH HOUR

FAINT and worn and aged
  One stands knocking at a gate;
Though no light shines in the casement,
  Knocking though so late.
  It has struck eleven
  In the courts of heaven,
Yet he still doth knock and wait.

  While no answer cometh
  From the heavenly hill,
  Blessed Angels wonder
  At his earnest will.
  Hope and fear but quicken
  While the shadows thicken:
He is knocking, knocking still.

  Grim the gate unopened
  Stands with bar and lock:
Yet within the unseen Porter
  Hearkens to the knock.—
  Doing and undoing,
  Faint and yet pursuing,
This man's feet are on the Rock.

  With a cry unceasing
  Knocketh, prayeth he:

THE ELEVENTH HOUR

"Lord have mercy on me
When I cry to Thee."
With a knock unceasing
And a cry increasing:
"O my Lord, remember me."

Still the Porter standeth,
Love-constrained He standeth near,
While the cry increaseth
Of that love and fear:
"Jesus, look upon me —
Christ, hast Thou foregone me? —
If I must, I perish here."

Faint the knocking ceases,
Faint the cry and call:
Is he lost indeed for ever,
Shut without the wall?
Mighty Arms surround him,
Arms that sought and found him,
Held, withheld, and bore through all.

O celestial mansion,
Open wide the door:
Crown and robes of whiteness,
Stone inscribed before,
Flocking Angels bear them;
Stretch thy hand and wear them,
Sit thou down for evermore.

5 *September* 1853.

FOR UNDER A CRUCIFIX

ONCE I ached for thy dear sake;
Wilt thou cause Me now to ache?
Once I bled for thee in pain;
Wilt thou pierce My Heart again?

Crown of thorns and shameful tree,
Bitter death I bore for thee,
Gave up glory, broke My will, —
And canst thou reject Me still?

WHO HAVE A FORM OF GODLINESS

WHEN I am sick and tired it is God's will:
Also God's will alone is sure and best: —
So in my weariness I find my rest,
And so in poverty I take my fill,
Therefore I see my good in midst of ill,
Therefore in loneliness I build my nest,
And through hot noon pant toward the shady west,
And hope in sickening disappointment still.
So, when the times of restitution come,
The sweet times of refreshing come at last,
My God shall fill my longings to the brim
Therefore I wait and look and long for Him:
Not wearied though the work is wearisome,
Nor fainting though the time be almost past.

18 *December* 1853.

THERE REMAINETH THEREFORE A REST

IN the grave will be no space
   For the purple of the proud —
   They must mingle with the crowd:
   In the wrappings of a shroud
Jewels would be out of place.

There no laughter shall be heard,
   Nor the heavy sound of sighs:
   Sleep shall seal the aching eyes:
   All the ancient and the wise
There shall utter not a word.

Yet it may be we shall hear
   How the mounting skylark sings
   And the bell for matins rings:
   Or perhaps the whisperings
Of white Angels sweet and clear.

What a calm when all is done,
   Wearing vigil, prayer, and fast!
   All fulfilled from first to last:
   All the length of time gone past
And eternity begun.

Fear and hope and chastening rod
   Urge us on the narrow way:

Bear we still as best we may
Heat and burden of the day,
Struggling, panting up to God.

17 *February* 1854.

YE HAVE FORGOTTEN THE EXHORTATION

ANGEL

BURY thy dead, dear friend,
Between the night and day:
Where depths of summer shade are cool,
And murmurs of a summer pool
And windy murmurs stray:—

SOUL

Ah gone away,
Ah dear and lost delight,
Gone from me and for ever out of sight!

ANGEL

Bury thy dead, dear love,
And make his bed most fair above:
The latest buds shall still
Blow there, and the first violets too,
And there a turtle-dove
Shall brood and coo:—

THE EXHORTATION

SOUL

I cannot make the nest
So warm but he may find it chill
In solitary rest.

ANGEL

Bury thy dead heart-deep:
Take patience till the sun be set:
There are no tears for him to weep,
No doubts to haunt him yet:
Take comfort, he will not forget: —

SOUL

Then I will watch beside his sleep:
Will watch alone,
And make my moan
Because the harvest is so long to reap.

ANGEL

The fields are white to harvest, look and see,
Are white abundantly.
The harvest-moon shines full and clear,
The harvest-time is near,
Be of good cheer: —

SOUL

Ah woe is me!
I have no heart for harvest-time,
Grown sick with hope deferred from chime to chime.

ANGEL

But One can give thee heart, thy Lord and his,
　　Can raise both thee and him
　　To shine with Seraphim,
And pasture where the eternal fountain is;
　　Can give thee of that tree
　　Whose leaves are health for thee;
　　Can give thee robes made clean and white,
　　And love, and all delight,
And beauty where the day turns not to night.
　　Who knocketh at His door,
　　And presseth in, goes out no more.
　　Kneel as thou hast not knelt before —
　　The time is short — and smite
Upon thy breast and pray with all thy might: —

SOUL

O Lord, my heart is broken for my sin:
　　Yet hasten Thine own day
　　And come away.
Is not time full? Oh put the sickle in,
　　O Lord, begin!

10 *May* 1854.

UNFORGOTTEN

O UNFORGOTTEN!
How long ago? one spirit saith.
As long as life even unto death,
The passage of a poor frail breath.

O unforgotten!
An unforgotten load of love,
A load of grief all griefs above,
A blank blank nest without its dove.

As long as time is: —
No longer? Time is but a span,
The dalliance-space of empty man:
And is this all immortals can?

Ever and ever,
Beyond all time, beyond all space:
Now shadows darkening heart and face;
Then glory in a glorious place.

Sad heart and spirit,
Bowed now, yea broken, for a while —
Lagging and toiling mile by mile,
Yet pressing toward the Eternal Smile.

O joy eternal!
O youth eternal without flaw! —
Thee not the blessed Angels saw,
Rapt in august adoring awe.

Not the dead have thee,
Not yet, O all-surpassing peace:
Not till this veiling world shall cease
And harvest yield its whole increase.

Not the dead know thee,
Not dead nor living nor unborn:
Who in the new-sown field at morn
Can measure out the harvest corn?—

Yet they shall know thee:
And we with them, and unborn men
With us, shall know and have thee when
The single grain shall wax to ten.

1855.

ZION SAID

O SLAIN for love of me, canst Thou be cold,
   Be cold and far away in my distress?
Is Thy love also changed, growing less and less,
That carried me through all the days of old?
O Slain for love of me, O Love untold,
   See how I flag and fail through weariness:
   I flag, while sleepless foes dog me and press
On me: behold, O Lord, O Love, behold!
I am sick for home, the home of love indeed—
   I am sick for Love, that dearest name for Thee:

Thou who hast bled, see how my heart doth bleed:
Open Thy bleeding Side and let me in:
Oh hide me in Thy Heart from doubt and sin,
Oh take me to Thyself and comfort me.

31 *December* 1855.

HYMN AFTER GABRIELE ROSSETTI

FIRST VERSION

T' amo e fra dolci affanni

MY Lord, my Love! in love's unrest
How often have I said,
"Blessed that John who on Thy breast
Reclined his head."
Thy touch it was, Love's Pelican,
Transformed him from above,
And made him amongst men the man
To show forth holy love.

Yet shall I envy blessed John?
Nay, not so verily,
While Thou indwellest as Thine own
Me, even me:
Upbuilding with Thy Manhood's worth
My frail humanity;
Yea Thy Divinehood pouring forth,
In fullness filling me.

Me, Lord, Thy temple consecrate,
  Me unto Thee alone;
Within my heart set up Thy state
  And mount Thy throne:
The Seraphim in ecstacy
  Fall prone around Thy house,
For which of them hath tasted Thee,
  My Manna and my Spouse?

Now Thou dost wear me for a robe
  And sway and warm me through,
I scarce seem lesser than the globe,
  Thy temple too:
O God, who for Thy dwelling-place
  Dost take delight in me,
The ungirt immensity of space
  Hath not encompassed Thee.

SECOND VERSION

My Lord, my Love! in pleasant pain
  How often have I said,
"Blessed that John who on Thy breast
  Laid down his head."
It was that contact all divine
  Transformed him from above,
And made him amongst men the man
  To show forth holy love.

Yet shall I envy blessed John?
　　Nay not so verily,
Now that Thou, Lord, both Man and God,
　　　Dost dwell in me:
Upbuilding with Thy Manhood's might
　　My frail humanity;
Yea, Thy Divinehood pouring forth,
　　In fullness filling me.

Me, Lord, Thy temple consecrate,
　　Even me to Thee alone;
Lord, reign upon my willing heart
　　　Which is Thy throne:
To Thee the Seraphim fall down
　　Adoring round Thy house;
For which of them hath tasted Thee,
　　My Manna and my Spouse?

Now that Thy life lives in my soul
　　And sways and warms it through,
I scarce seem lesser than the world,
　　Thy temple too.
O God, who dwellest in my heart,
　　My God who fillest me,
The broad immensity itself
　　Hath not encompassed Thee.

Circa 1855.

HOW LONG?

MY life is long — Not so the Angels say
 Who watch me waste it, trembling whilst they
   weigh
Against eternity my lavished day.

My life is long — Not so the Saints in peace
Judge, filled with plenitude that cannot cease:
Oh life was short which bought such large increase!

My life is long — Christ's word is different:
The heat and burden of the day were spent
On Him, — to me refreshing times are sent.

Give me an Angel's heart, that day nor night
Rests not from adoration its delight,
Still crying "Holy holy" in the height.

Give me the heart of Saints, who, laid at rest
In better Paradise than Abraham's breast,
In the everlasting Rock have made their nest.

Give me Thy heart, O Christ, who thirty-three
Slow years of sorrow countedst short for me,
That where Thou art there Thy beloved might be.

14 *April* 1856.

A MARTYR

IT is over the horrible pain,
　　All is over the struggle and doubt:
She's asleep though her friends stand and weep,
　　She's asleep while the multitudes shout:
Not to wake to her anguish again,
　　Not to wake until death is cast out.

Stoop, look at the beautiful face,
　　See the smile on the satisfied mouth,
The hands crost — she hath conquered not lost:
　　She hath drunk who was fevered with drouth:
She shall sleep in her safe resting-place
　　While the hawk spreads her wings toward the South.

She shall sleep while slow seasons are given,
　　While daylight and darkness go round:
Her heart is at rest in its nest,
　　Her body at rest in the ground:
She has travelled the long road to heaven,
　　She sought it and now she has found.

Will you follow the track that she trod,
　　Will you tread in her footsteps, my friend?
That pathway is rough, but enough
　　Are the light and the balm that attend.
Do I tread in her steps, O my God,—
　　Shall I joy with her joy in the end?

23 *April* 1856.

NOW THEY DESIRE

THERE is a sleep we have not slept,
  Safe in a bed unknown:
There hearts are staunched that long have wept
  Alone or bled alone:
Sweet sleep that dreams not, or whose dream
  Is foretaste of the truth:
Sweet sleep whose sweets are what they seem,
  Refreshing more than youth.

There is a sea whose waters clear
  Are never tempest-tost:
There is a home whose children dear
  Are saved, not one is lost:
There Cherubim and Seraphim
  And Angels dwell with Saints,
Whose lustre no more dwindleth dim,
  Whose ardour never faints.

There is a Love which fills desire
  And can our love requite:
Like fire it draws our lesser fire,
  Like greater light our light:
For it we agonize in strife,
  We yearn, we famish thus —
Lo in the far-off land of life
  Doth it not yearn for us?

O fair, O fair Jerusalem,
   How fair, how far away,
When shall we see thy Jasper-gem
   That gives thee light for day?
Thy sea of glass like fire, thy streets
   Of glass like virgin gold,
Thy royal Elders on their seats,
   Thy four Beasts manifold?

Fair City of delights, the bride
   In raiment white and clean,
When shall we see the loving-eyed,
   Sun-girdled, happy Queen?
Without a wrinkle or a spot,
   Blood-cleansed, blood-purchased once:
In how fair ground is fallen the lot
   Of all thy happy sons!

Dove's eyes beneath thy parted lock,
   A dove's soft voice is thine:
Thy nest is safe within the Rock,
   Safe in the very Vine:
Thy walls salvation buildeth them
   And all thy gates are praise,
O fair, O fair Jerusalem,
   In sevenfold day of days.

13 *August* 1856.

A CHRISTMAS CAROL

For my Godchildren

THE Shepherds had an Angel,
    The Wise Men had a star,
But what have I, a little child,
    To guide me home from far,
Where glad stars sing together
    And singing angels are?—

Lord Jesus is my Guardian,
    So I can nothing lack:
The lambs lie in His bosom
    Along life's dangerous track:
The wilful lambs that go astray
    He bleeding fetches back.

Lord Jesus is my guiding star,
    My beacon-light in heaven:
He leads me step by step along
    The path of life uneven:
He, true light, leads me to that land
    Whose day shall be as seven.

Those Shepherds through the lonely night
    Sat watching by their sheep,

A CHRISTMAS CAROL

Until they saw the heavenly host
    Who neither tire nor sleep,
All singing "Glory glory"
    In festival they keep.

Christ watches me, His little lamb,
    Cares for me day and night,
That I may be His own in heaven:
    So angels clad in white
Shall sing their "Glory glory"
    For my sake in the height.

The Wise Men left their country
    To journey morn by morn,
With gold and frankincense and myrrh,
    Because the Lord was born:
God sent a star to guide them
    And sent a dream to warn.

My life is like their journey,
    Their star is like God's book,
I must be like those good Wise Men
    With heavenward heart and look:
But shall I give no gifts to God? —
    What precious gifts they took!

Lord, I will give my love to Thee,
    Than gold much costlier,
Sweeter to Thee than frankincense,
    More prized than choicest myrrh:

Lord, make me dearer day by day,
    Day by day holier;

Nearer and dearer by day:
    Till I my voice unite,
    And sing my "Glory glory"
        With angels clad in white;
All "Glory glory" given to Thee
    Through all the heavenly height.

6 *October* 1856.

NOT YOURS BUT YOU

"HE died for me: what can I offer Him?
    Toward Him swells incense of perpetual
        prayer:
His court wear crowns and aureoles round their
    hair:
His ministers are subtle Cherubim;
Ring within ring, white intense Seraphim
    Leap like immortal lightnings through the air.
What shall I offer Him? defiled and bare,
My spirit broken and my brightness dim." —
"Give Me thy youth." — "I yield it to Thy rod,
    As Thou didst yield Thy prime of youth for me." —
    "Give Me thy life." — "I give it breath by breath,
    As Thou didst give Thy life so give I Thee." —
"Give Me thy love." — "So be it, my God, my God,
    As Thou hast loved me even to bitter death."

27 *October* 1856.

THE HEART KNOWETH ITS OWN BITTERNESS

WHEN all the over-work of life
    Is finished once, and fast asleep
We swerve no more beneath the knife
    But taste that silence cool and deep;
Forgetful of the highways rough,
    Forgetful of the thorny scourge,
    Forgetful of the tossing surge,
Then shall we find it is enough?

How can we say "enough" on earth —
    "Enough" with such a craving heart?
I have not found it since my birth,
    But still have bartered part for part.
I have not held and hugged the whole,
    But paid the old to gain the new:
    Much have I paid, yet much is due,
Till I am beggared sense and soul.

I used to labour, used to strive
    For pleasure with a restless will:
Now if I save my soul alive
    All else what matters, good or ill?
I used to dream alone, to plan
    Unspoken hopes and days to come: —
    Of all my past this is the sum —
I will not lean on child of man.

HEART'S BITTERNESS

To give, to give, not to receive!
　　I long to pour myself, my soul,
Not to keep back or count or leave,
　　But king with king to give the whole.
I long for one to stir my deep —
　　I have had enough of help and gift —
　　I long for one to search and sift
Myself, to take myself and keep.

You scratch my surface with your pin,
　　You stroke me smooth with hushing breath: —
Nay pierce, nay probe, nay dig within,
　　Probe my quick core and sound my depth.
You call me with a puny call,
　　You talk, you smile, you nothing do:
　　How should I spend my heart on you,
My heart that so outweighs you all?

Your vessels are by much too strait:
　　Were I to pour, you could not hold. —
Bear with me: I must bear to wait,
　　A fountain sealed through heat and cold.
Bear with me days or months or years:
　　Deep must call deep until the end
　　When friend shall no more envy friend
Nor vex his friend at unawares.

Not in this world of hope deferred,
　　This world of perishable stuff: —
Eye hath not seen nor ear hath heard
　　Nor heart conceived that full "enough":

Here moans the separating sea,
　　Here harvests fail, here breaks the heart:
　　There God shall join and no man part,
I full of Christ and Christ of me.

27 August 1857.

A BURDEN

THEY lie at rest asleep and dead,
　　The dew is cool above their head,
They knew not when past summer fled —
　　　　　　　　　　Amen.

They lie at rest and quite forget
The hopes and fears that wring us yet:
Their eyes are set, their heart is set —
　　　　　　　　　　Amen.

They lie with us, yet gone away
Hear nothing that we sob or say
Beneath the thorn of wintry May —
　　　　　　　　　　Miserere.

They lie asleep with us, and take
Sweet rest although our heart should ache,
Rest on although our heart should break —
　　　　　　　　　　Miserere.

Together all yet each alone,
Each laid at rest beneath his own
Smooth turf or white appointed stone —
                        Amen.

When shall our slumbers be so deep,
And bleeding heart and eyes that weep
Lie lapped in the sufficient sleep? —
                        Miserere.

We dream of them, and who shall say
They never dream while far away
Of us between the night and day? —
                      Sursum Corda.

Gone far away: or it may be
They lean toward us and hear and see,
Yea and remember more than we —
                        Amen.

For wherefore should we think them far
Who know not where those spirits are
That shall be glorious as a star? —
                        Hallelujah.

Where chill or change can never rise,
Deep in the depth of Paradise
They rest world-wearied heart and eyes —
                        Jubilate.

Safe as a hidden brooding dove,
With perfect peace within, above,
They love, and look for perfect love —
                    Hallelujah.

We hope and love with throbbing breast,
They hope and love and are at rest:
And yet we question which is best —
                    Miserere.

Oh what is earth, that we should build
Our houses here, and seek concealed
Poor treasure, and add field to field

And heap to heap and store to store,
Still grasping more and seeking more
While Death stands knocking at the door? —
                    Cui bono?

But one will answer: Changed and pale
And sick at heart, I thirst, I fail
For love, I thirst without avail —
                    Miserrima.

Sweet love, a fountain sealed to me:
Sweet love, the one sufficiency
For all the longings that can be —
                    Amen.

Oh happy they alone whose lot
Is love!   I search from spot to spot:
In life, in death, I find it not —
                    Miserrima.

Not found in life: nay verily.
I too have sought: come sit with me,
And grief for grief shall answer thee —
                        Miserrima.

Sit with me where the sapless leaves
Are heaped and sere: to him who grieves
What cheer have last year's harvest-sheaves? —
                        Cui bono?

Not found in life yet found in death.
Hush, throbbing heart and sobbing breath!
There is a nest of love beneath

The sod, a home prepared before:
Our brethren whom one mother bore
Live there, and toil and ache no more —
                        Hallelujah.

Our friends, our kinsfolk, great and small,
Our loved, our best beloved of all,
They watch across the parting wall

(Do they not watch?) and count the creep
Of time, and sound the shallowing deep,
Till we in port shall also sleep —
                        Hallelujah, Amen.

16 *July* 1858.

ONLY BELIEVE

I STOOD by weeping
 Yet a sorrowful silence keeping
While an Angel smote my love
 As she lay sleeping.

"Is there a bed above
 More fragrant than these violets
That are white like death?"

"White like a dove,
Flowers in the blessed islets
 Breathe sweeter breath
All fair morns and twilights."

"Is the gold there
More golden than these tresses?"

"There heads are aureoled
 And crowned like gold
 With light most rare."

"Are the bowers of Heaven
 More choice than these?"

"To them are given
All odorous shady trees

Earth's bowers are wildernesses,
Compared with the recesses
    Made soft there now
Nest-like twixt bough and bough."

"Who shall live in such a nest?"

"Heart with heart at rest:
All they whose troubles cease
    In peace:
    Souls that wrestled
    Now are nestled
    There at ease, —
Throng from east and west,
    From north and south,
To plenty from the land of drouth."

September 1858.

A SHADOW OF DOROTHEA

"GOLDEN-HAIRED, lily-white,
    Will you pluck me lilies?
Or will you show me where they grow,
    Show where the summer rill is?
But is your hair of gold or light,
And is your foot of flake or fire,
And have you wings rolled up from sight,
    And joy to slake desire?"

"I pluck young flowers of Paradise,
　　Lilies and roses red:
　　A sceptre for my hand,
A crown to crown my golden head.
　　Love makes me wise:
　　I sing, I stand,
I pluck palm-branches in the sheltered land."

"Is there a path to heaven
　　My heavy foot may tread?
And will you show that way to go,
　　That rose and lily bed?
　　Which day of all these seven
　　Will lighten my heart of lead,
Will purge mine eyes and make me wise,
　　Alive or dead?"

"There is a heavenward stair—
Mount, strain upwards, strain and strain—
Each step will crumble to your foot
That never shall descend again.
There grows a tree from ancient root
With healing leaves and twelvefold fruit
　　In musical heaven-air:
　　Feast with me there."

"I have a home on earth I cannot leave,
I have a friend on earth I cannot grieve:
Come down to me, I cannot mount to you."

"Nay, choose between us both,
Choose as you are lief or loth:
You cannot keep these things and have me too."

11 November 1858.

FOR HENRIETTA POLYDORE

ON the land and on the sea
Jesus keep both you and me:

Going out and coming in,
Christ keep us both from shame and sin:

In this world, in the world to come,
Keep us safe and lead us home:

To-day in toil, to-night in rest,
Be best beloved and love us best.

16 January 1859.

ASH WEDNESDAY

JESUS, do I love Thee?
Thou art far above me,
Seated out of sight,
Hid in heavenly light
Of most highest height.

ASH WEDNESDAY

Martyred hosts implore Thee,
Seraphs fall before Thee,
Angels and Archangels,
Cherub throngs adore Thee.
Blessed she that bore Thee!
All the saints approve Thee,
All the virgins love Thee.
I show as a blot
Blood hath cleansèd not,
As a barren spot
In thy fruitful lot;
I, fig-tree fruit-unbearing,
Thou, righteous Judge unsparing:
What canst Thou do more to me
That shall not more undo me?
Thy Justice hath a sound,
"Why cumbereth it the ground?"
Thy Love with stirrings stronger
Pleads, "Give it one year longer."
Thou giv'st me time: but who
Save Thou shall give me dew,
Shall feed my root with blood
And stir my sap for good? —
Oh by Thy gifts that shame me
Give more lest they condemn me.
Good Lord, I ask much of Thee,
But most I ask to love Thee:
Kind Lord, be mindful of me,
Love me and make me love Thee.

21 *March* 1859.

A CHRISTMAS CAROL

BEFORE the paling of the stars,
  Before the winter morn,
Before the earliest cock-crow
Jesus Christ was born:
  Born in a stable
  Cradled in a manger,
In the world His hands had made
  Born a stranger.

Priest and King lay fast asleep
  In Jerusalem,
Young and old lay fast asleep
  In crowded Bethlehem:
Saint and Angel, ox and ass,
  Kept a watch together,
Before the Christmas daybreak
  In the winter weather.

Jesus on His Mother's breast
  In the stable cold,
Spotless Lamb of God was He,
  Shepherd of the fold:
Let us kneel with Mary Maid,
  With Joseph bent and hoary,
With Saint and Angel, ox and ass,
  To hail the King of Glory.

26 *August* 1859.

EASTER EVEN

THERE is nothing more that they can do
    For all their rage and boast:
Caiaphas with his blaspheming crew,
    Herod with his host;

Pontius Pilate in his judgment hall
    Judging their Judge and his,
Or he who led them all and past them all,
    Arch-Judas with his kiss.

The sepulchre made sure with ponderous stone,
    Seal that same stone, O priest:
It may be thou shalt block the Holy One
    From rising in the east.

Set a watch about the sepulchre
    To watch on pain of death:
They must hold fast the stone if One should stir
    And shake it from beneath.

God Almighty, He can break a seal,
    And roll away a stone:
Can grind the proud in dust who would not kneel,
    And crush the mighty one.

There is nothing more that they can do
   For all their passionate care,
Those who sit in dust, the blessed few,
   And weep and rend their hair.

Peter, Thomas, Mary Magdalen,
   The Virgin unreproved,
Joseph and Nicodemus foremost men,
   And John the well-beloved.

Bring your finest linen and your spice,
   Swathe the sacred Dead,
Bind with careful hands and piteous eyes
   The napkin round His head:

Lay Him in the garden-rock to rest:
   Rest you the Sabbath length:
The Sun that went down crimson in the west
   Shall rise renewed in strength.

God Almighty shall give joy for pain,
   Shall comfort him who grieves:
Lo He with joy shall doubtless come again
   And with Him bring His sheaves.

23 *March* 1861.

THE OFFERING OF THE NEW LAW

ONCE I thought to sit so high
In the palace of the sky:
Now I thank God for His grace
If I may fill the lowest place.

Once I thought to scale so soon
Heights above the changing moon:
Now I thank God for delay: —
To-day: it yet is called to-day.

While I stumble, halt and blind,
Lo He waiteth to be kind:
Bless me soon or bless me slow —
Except He bless I let not go.

Once for earth I laid my plan,
Once I leaned on strength of man:
When my hope was swept aside
I stayed my broken heart on pride:

Broken reed hath pierced my hand,
Fell my house I built on sand,
Roofless, wounded, maimed by sin,
Fightings without and fears within.

Yet, His tree, He feeds my root:
Yet, His branch, He prunes for fruit:
Yet, His sheep, these eves and morns
He seeks for me among the thorns.

With Thine Image stamped of old,
Find Thy coin more choice than gold:
Known to Thee by name, recall
To Thee Thy homesick prodigal.

Sacrifice and offering
None there is that I can bring —
None save what is Thine alone:
I bring Thee, Lord, but of Thine own.

Broken Body, Blood outpoured,
These I bring, my God, my Lord;
Wine of Life and Living Bread,
With these for me Thy board is spread.

23 *May* 1861.

BY THE WATERS OF BABYLON

BY the waters of Babylon
   We sit down and weep,
Far from the pleasant land
   Where our fathers sleep:
Far from our Holy Place
   From which the Glory is gone:

We sit in dust and weep
By the waters of Babylon.

By the waters of Babylon
　The willow-trees grow rank:
We hang our harps thereon
　Silent upon the bank.
Before us the days are dark,
　And dark the days that are gone:
We grope in the very dark
　By the waters of Babylon.

By the waters of Babylon
　We thirst for Jordan yet,
We pine for Jerusalem
　Whereon our hearts are set:
Our priests defiled and slain,
　Our princes ashamed and gone,
Oh how should we forget
　By the waters of Babylon?

By the waters of Babylon
　Though the wicked grind the just,
Our seed shall yet strike root
　And shall shoot up from the dust;
The captive shall lead captive,
　The slave rise up and begone,
And thou too shalt sit in dust,
　O daughter of Babylon.

1 *December* 1861.

WITHIN THE VEIL

SHE holds a lily in her hand,
  Where long ranks of Angels stand:
A silver lily for her wand.

All her hair falls sweeping down,
Her hair that is a golden brown,
A crown beneath her golden crown.

Blooms a rose-bush at her knee,
Good to smell and good to see:
It bears a rose for her, for me:

Her rose a blossom richly grown,
My rose a bud not fully blown
But sure one day to be mine own.

13 *December* 1861.

OUT OF THE DEEP

HAVE mercy, Thou my God — mercy, my God!
  For I can hardly bear life day by day.
Be I here or there, I fret myself away:
Lo for Thy staff I have but felt Thy rod
Along this tedious desert-path long trod.
  When will Thy judgment judge me, yea or nay?
  I pray for grace; but then my sins unpray
My prayer: on holy ground I fool stand shod —

While still Thou haunt'st me, faint upon the cross,
   A sorrow beyond sorrow in Thy look,
   Unutterable craving for my soul.
All-faithful Thou, Lord: I, not Thou, forsook
   Myself: I traitor slunk back from the goal:
Lord, I repent — help Thou my helpless loss.

17 *December* 1862.

FOR A MERCY RECEIVED

THANK God who spared me what I feared!
   Once more I gird myself to run.
Thy promise stands, Thou Faithful One.
Horror of darkness disappeared
   At length: once more I see the sun,

And dare to wait in hope for Spring,
   To face and bear the Winter's cold:
   The dead cocoon shall yet unfold
And give to light the living wing:
   There's hidden sap beneath the mould.

My God, how could my courage flag
   So long as Thou art still the same?
   For what were labour, failure, shame,
Whilst Thy sure promise doth not lag,
   And Thou dost shield me with Thy Name?

FOR A MERCY RECEIVED

Yet am I weak, my faith is weak,
   My heart is weak that pleads with Thee:
O Thou that art not far to seek,
Turn to me, hearken when I speak,
   Stretch forth Thy hand to succour me.

Through many perils have I past,
   Deaths, plagues, and wonders, have I seen:
Till now Thy hand hath held me fast:
Lord, help me, hold me, to the last:
   Still be what Thou hast always been.

Open Thy Heart of Love to me,
   Give me Thyself, keep nothing back,
Even as I give myself to Thee.
   Love paid by love doth nothing lack,
   And Love to pay love is not slack.

Love doth so grace and dignify
   That beggars sue as king with king
Before the Throne of Grace on high:
My God, be gracious to my cry:
   My God, accept what gift I bring: —

A heart that loves: though soiled and bruised,
   Yet chosen by Thee in time of yore.
Who ever came and was refused
By Thee? Do, Lord, as Thou art used
   To do, and make me love Thee more.

13 January 1863.

CONFERENCE BETWEEN CHRIST, THE SAINTS, AND THE SOUL

I AM pale with sick desire,
   For my heart is far away
From this world's fitful fire
   And this world's waning day;
In a dream it overleaps
   A world of tedious ills
To where the sunshine sleeps
   On the everlasting hills.
Say the Saints — "There Angels ease us,
   Glorified and white."
   They say — "We rest in Jesus,
Where is not day nor night."

   My Soul saith — "I have sought
     For a home that is not gained;
I have spent yet nothing bought,
   Have laboured but not attained;
My pride strove to rise and grow,
   And hath but dwindled down;
My love sought love, and lo
   Hath not attained its crown."
Say the Saints — "Fresh souls increase us,
   None languish nor recede."
   They say — "We love our Jesus,
And He loves us indeed."

CHRIST, THE SAINTS, AND THE SOUL

    I cannot rise above,
        I cannot rest beneath,
    I cannot find out love,
        Nor escape from death;
    Dear hopes and joys gone by
        Still mock me with a name;
    My best-beloved die
        And I cannot die with them.
Say the Saints — "No deaths decrease us,
Where our rest is glorious."
    They say — "We live in Jesus,
Who once died for us."

    Oh my Soul she beats her wings,
        And pants to fly away
    Up to immortal things
        In the heavenly day.
Yet she flags and almost faints;
        Can such be meant for me?
"Come and see" — say the Saints.
        Saith Jesus — "Come and see."
Say the Saints — "His pleasures please us
    Before God and the Lamb."
"Come and taste My sweets" — saith Jesus —
    "Be with Me where I am."

Circa 1863.

COME UNTO ME

OH for the time gone by when thought of Christ
    Made His yoke easy and His burden light!
When my heart stirred within me at the sight
Of altar spread for awful Eucharist:
When all my hopes His promises sufficed:
    When my soul watched for Him, by day, by night:
    When my lamp lightened and my robe was white,
And all seemed loss except the pearl unpriced.
Yet, since He calls me still with tender call,
    Since He remembers whom I half forgot,
    I even will run my race and bear my lot:
    For Faith the walls of Jericho cast down,
    And Hope to whoso runs holds forth a crown,
And Love is Christ, and Christ is all in all.

23 February 1864.

IN PATIENCE

I WILL not faint, but trust in God
    Who this my lot hath given:
He leads me by the thorny road
    Which is the road to heaven.
Though sad my day that lasts so long,
At evening I shall have a song:
Though dim my day until the night,
At evening-time there shall be light.

My life is but a working day
  Whose tasks are set aright:
A while to work, a while to pray
  And then a quiet night.
And then, please God, a quiet night
Where Saints and Angels walk in white:
One dreamless sleep from work and sorrow,
But re-awakening on the morrow.

19 *March* 1864.

NONE WITH HIM

MY God, to live: how didst Thou bear to live,
  Preaching and teaching, toiling to and fro?
Few men accepting what Thou hadst to give,
    Few men prepared to know
Thy face, to see the truth Thou cam'st to show.

My God, to die: how didst Thou bear to die
  That long slow death in weariness of pain?
A curse and an astonishment, past by,
    Pointed at, mocked again,
By men for whom Thy blood was shed in vain.

Whilst I do hardly bear my easy life,
  And hardly face my easy-coming death:
I turn to flee before the tug of strife;
    And shrink with troubled breath
From sleep, that is not death, Thy Spirit saith.

14 *June* 1864.

BIRDS OF PARADISE

GOLDEN-WINGED, silver-winged,
　　Winged with flashing flame,
Such a flight of birds I saw,
　　Birds without a name:
Singing songs in their own tongue —
　　Song of songs — they came.

　　One to another calling,
　　　　Each answering each,
　　One to another calling,
　　　　In their proper speech:
High above my head they wheeled,
　　　　Far out of reach.

On wings of flame they went and came
　　With a cadenced clang:
　　Their silver wings tinkled,
　　Their golden wings rang;
The wind it whistled through their wings
　　Where in heaven they sang.

　　They flashed and they darted
　　　　Awhile before mine eyes,
　　Mounting, mounting, mounting still,
　　　　In haste to scale the skies,
Birds without a nest on earth,
　　Birds of Paradise.

s

Where the moon riseth not
Nor sun seeks the west,
There to sing their glory
Which they sing at rest,
There to sing their love-song
When they sing their best: —

Not in any garden
That mortal foot hath trod,
Not in any flowering tree
That springs from earthly sod,
But in the garden where they dwell,
The Paradise of God.

14 November 1864.

I KNOW YOU NOT

O CHRIST, the Vine with living fruit,
    The twelvefold-fruited Tree of Life,
The Balm in Gilead after strife,
    The Valley-lily and the Rose;
Stronger than Lebanon, Thou Root;
Sweeter than clustered grapes, Thou Vine;
O best, Thou Vineyard of red wine,
    Keeping Thy best wine till the close.

Pearl of great price Thyself alone,
    And ruddier than the ruby Thou;

I KNOW YOU NOT

Most precious lightning Jasper stone,
Head of the corner spurned before:
Fair gate of pearl, Thyself the Door;
Clear golden street, Thyself the Way;
  By Thee we journey toward Thee now,
Through Thee shall enter heaven one day.

I thirst for Thee, full fount and flood;
  My heart calls Thine, as deep to deep:
    Dost Thou forget Thy sweat and pain,
    Thy provocation on the cross?
  Heart-pierced for me, vouchsafe to keep
The purchase of Thy lavished Blood:
  The gain is Thine, Lord, if I gain;
    Or, if I lose, Thine own the loss.

At midnight, saith the Parable,
  A cry was made, the Bridegroom came;
    Those who were ready entered in:
  The rest, shut out in death and shame,
    Strove all too late that feast to win,
  Their die was cast, and fixed their lot;
A gulf divided heaven from hell;
  The Bridegroom said — I know you not.

But Who is this that shuts the door,
  And saith — I know you not — to them?
    I see the wounded hands and side,
    The brow thorn-tortured long ago:

Yea, This who grieved and bled and died,
This same is He who must condemn;
He called, but they refused to know;
So now He hears their cry no more.

Circa 1864.

THOU ART THE SAME AND THY YEARS SHALL NOT FAIL

THE flowers that bloom in sun and shade,
   And glitter in the dew —
     The flowers must fade.
The birds that build their nest and sing
   When lovely Spring is new .
     Must soon take wing.

The sun that rises in his strength,
   To wake and warm the world,
     Must set at length.
The sea that overflows the shore
   With billows frothed and curled
     Must ebb once more.

All come and go, all wax and wane,
   O Lord, save only Thou,
     Who dost remain
The same to all eternity.
   All things which fail us now
     We trust to Thee   Amen.

Circa 1880.

A CHRISTMAS CAROL

WHOSO hears a chiming for Christmas at the nighest
Hears a sound like Angels chanting in their glee,
Hears a sound like palm-boughs waving in the highest,
Hears a sound like ripple of a crystal sea.
Sweeter than a prayer-bell for a saint in dying,
Sweeter than a death-bell for a saint at rest,
Music struck in heaven, with earth's faint replying,
"Life is good and death is good, for Christ is best."

Circa 1886.

CARDINAL NEWMAN

In the grave, whither thou goest

O WEARY Champion of the Cross, lie still:
Sleep thou at length the all-embracing sleep:
Long was thy sowing-day, rest now and reap:
Thy fast was long, feast now thy spirit's fill.
Yea take thy fill of love, because thy will
Chose love not in the shallows but the deep:
Thy tides were spring-tides, set against the neap
Of calmer souls: thy flood rebuked their rill.

Now night has come to thee — please God, of rest:
   So some time must it come to every man;
      To first and last, where many last are first.
   Now fixed and finished thine eternal plan,
      Thy best has done its best, thy worst its worst:
Thy best its best, please God, thy best its best.

16 *August* 1890.

YEA I HAVE A GOODLY HERITAGE

MY vineyard that is mine I have to keep,
   Pruning for fruit the pleasant twigs and leaves.
Tend thou thy cornfield: one day thou shalt reap
   In joy thy ripened sheaves.

Or, if thine be an orchard, graft and prop
   Food-bearing trees each watered in its place:
Or, if a garden, let it yield for crop
   Sweet herbs and herb of grace. —

But if my lot be sand where nothing grows? —
   Nay who hath said it? Tune a thankful psalm:
For, though thy desert bloom not as the rose,
   It yet can rear thy palm.

Circa 1890.

A DEATH OF A FIRST-BORN

14 January 1892

ONE young life lost, two happy young lives blighted,
    With earthward eyes we see:
With eyes uplifted, keener, farther-sighted,
    We look, O Lord, to Thee.

Grief hears a funeral knell: Hope hears the ringing
    Of birthday bells on high;
Faith, Hope, and Love, make answer with soft singing,
    Half carol and half cry.

Stoop to console us, Christ, sole consolation,
    While dust returns to dust;
Until that blessed day when all Thy nation
    Shall rise up of the Just.

January 1892.

FAINT YET PURSUING

I

BEYOND this shadow and this turbulent sea,
    Shadow of death and turbulent sea of death,
Lies all we long to have or long to be.
    Take heart, tired man, toil on with lessening breath,
Lay violent hands on heaven's high treasury,
    Be what you long to be through life-long scathe.
A little while Hope leans on Charity,
    A little while Charity heartens Faith:
A little while: and then what further while?
    One while that ends not and that wearies not,
        For ever new whilst evermore the same.
    All things made new bear each a sweet new name;
        Man's lot of death has turned to life his lot,
And tearful Charity to Love's own smile.

II

Press onward, quickened souls, who mounting move,
    Press onward, upward, fire with mounting fire;
    Gathering volume of untold desire,
Press upward, homeward, dove with mounting dove.
Point me the excellent way that leads above;
    Woo me with sequent will, me too to aspire;
    With sequent heart to follow higher and higher,
To follow all who follow on to Love.

Up the high steep, across the golden sill,
  Up out of shadows into very light,
    Up out of dwindling life to life aglow,
  I watch you, my beloved, out of sight;—
Sight fails me, and my heart is watching still:
    My heart fails, yet I follow on to know.

Circa 1892.

HEAVEN OVERARCHES

HEAVEN overarches earth and sea,
    Earth-sadness and sea-bitterness.
Heaven overarches you and me:
A little while and we shall be—
Please God—where there is no more sea
    Nor barren wilderness.

Heaven overarches you and me,
  And all earth's gardens and her graves.
Look up with me, until we see
The day break and the shadows flee.
What though to-night wrecks you and me
    If so to-morrow saves?

Circa 1893.

ITALIAN POEMS

VERSI

FIGLIA, la Madre disse,
    Guardati dall' Amore:
È crudo, è traditore —
    Che vuoi saper di più?
Non fargli mai sperare
D' entrare nel tuo petto,
Chè chi gli dà ricetto
    Sempre tradito fu.

Colla sua benda al ciglio
È un bel fanciullo, è vero:
Ma sempre è menzognero,
    Ma sempre tradirà.
Semplice tu se fidi
Nel riso suo fallace;
Tu perderai la pace,
    Nè mai ritornerà.

Ma vedo — già sai stanca
Del mio parlar prudente;
Già volgi nella mente
    Il quando, il come, e il chi;
Odimi: i detti miei
Già sai se son sinceri —
E se son falsi o veri
    Saprai per prova un dì.

6 *Ottobre* 1849.

L' INCOGNITA

NOBIL rosa ancor non crebbe
  Senza spine in sullo stelo:
Se vi fosse, allor sarebbe
    Atta immagine di te.
  È la luna in mezzo al cielo
Bella è ver ma passeggiera:
Passa ancor la primavera: —
    Ah l' immagin tua dov' è?

Circa 1850.

NIGELLA

PURPUREA rosa,
  Dolce, odorosa,
È molto bella —
  Ma pur non è,
  O mia Nigella,
  Rival di te.

Donna nel velo,
Fior sullo stelo,
Ciascun l' amore
  Reclama a sè;
Ma passa il fiore —
  Tu resti a me.

Circa 1850.

CHIESA E SIGNORE

La Chiesa

VOLA, preghiera, e digli
   Perchè Ti stai lontano?
Passeggi Tu frai gigli
   Portando rosa in mano?
Non Ti fui giglio e rosa
   Quando mi amasti Tu?
Rivolgiti alla sposa,
   O mio Signor Gesù.

Il Signore

Di te non mi scordai
   Sposa mia dolce e mesta:
Se Mi sei rosa il sai,
   Chè porto spine in testa.
Ti diedi e core e vita,
   Me tutto Io diedi a te,
Ed or ti porgo aita:
   Abbi fidanza in Me.

La Chiesa

Vola, preghiera, a Lui,
   E grida: Ahi pazienza!

Te voglio e non altrui,
Te senza è tutto senza.
Fragrante più di giglio
E rosa a me sei Tu,
Di Dio l' Eterno Figlio,
O mio Signor Gesù.

Circa 1860.

IL ROSSEGGIAR DELL' ORIENTE

Canzoniere all' Amico lontano

I

AMOR DORMENTE

ADDIO, diletto amico;
 A me non lece amore,
Chè già m' uccise il core
 Amato amante.
Eppur per l' altra vita
 Consacro a te speranze;
Per questa, rimembranze
 Tante e poi tante.

Dicembre 1862.

2

Amor si sveglia?

IN nuova primavera
   Rinasce il genio antico;
Amor t' insinua "Spera" —
   Pur io nol dico.

S' "Ama" ti dice Amore,
   S' ei t' incoraggia, amico,
Giurando " È tuo quel core " —
   Pur io nol dico.

Anzi quel cor davvero
   Chi sa se valga un fico?
Lo credo, almen lo spero;
   Ma pur nol dico.

Gennaio 1863.

3

Si rimanda la tocca-caldaja

LUNGI da me il pensiere
   D' ereditar l' oggetto
Ch' una fiata in petto
   Destar ti seppe amor.
Se più l' usar non vuoi,
   Se pur fumar nol puoi,
Dolce ti sia dovere
   Il conservarlo ognor.

4

BLUMINE RISPONDE

S' IO t' incontrassi nell' eterna pace,
    Pace non più, per me saria diletto;
S' io t' incontrassi in cerchio maledetto,
Te più di me lamenterei verace.
Per te mia vita mezzo morta giace,
    Per te le notti veglio e bagno il letto:
Eppur di rivederti un dì m' aspetto
In secol che riman, non che in fugace.
E perciò "Fuggi" io dico al tempo; e omai
"Passa pur" dico al vanitoso mondo.
Mentre mi sogno quel che dici e fai
    Ripeto in me, "Doman sarà giocondo,
Doman sarem" — ma s' ami tu lo sai,
    E se non ami a che mostrarti il fondo?

Gennaio 1867.

5

Lassù fia caro il rivederci

DOLCE cor mio perduto e non perduto,
    Dolce mia vita che mi lasci in morte,
Amico e più che amico, ti saluto.
    Ricordati di me; chè cieche e corte
Fur le speranze mie, ma furon tue:
    Non disprezzar questa mia dura sorte.

Lascia ch' io dica "Le speranze sue
 Come le mie languiro in questo inverno"—
Pur mi rassegnerò, quel che fue fue.
 Lascia ch' io dica ancor, "Con lui discerno
Giorno che spunta da gelata sera,
 Lungo cielo al di là di breve inferno,
Al di là dell' inverno primavera."

Gennaio 1867.

6

Non son io la rosa ma vi stetti appresso

CASA felice ove più volte omai
 Siede il mio ben parlando e ancor ridendo,
 Donna felice che con lui sedendo
Lo allegri pur con quanto dici e fai,
Giardin felice dove passeggiai
 Pensando a lui, pensando e non dicendo,—
 Giorno felice fia quand' io mi rendo
Laddove passeggiando a lui pensai.
 Ma s' egli vi sarà quand' io vi torno,
 S' egli m' accoglie col suo dolce riso,
Ogni uccelletto canterà dintorno,
 La rosa arrossirà nel vago viso:—
Iddio ci dia in eternità quel giorno,
 Ci dia per quel giardino il paradiso.

Aprile 1867.

7

Lassuso il caro Fiore

SE t' insegnasse Iddio
　Il proprio Amor così,
Ti cederei, cor mio,
　Al caro Fiore.
Il caro Fior ti chiama,
　"Fammi felice un dì";—
Il caro Fior che t' ama
　Ti chiede amore.

Quel Fiore in paradiso
　Fiorisce ognor per te;
Sì, rivedrai quel viso,
　Sarai contento:
Intorno al duol ch' è stato
　Domanderai "Dov' è?"
Chè passerà il passato
　In un momento.

Ed io per tanta vista
　In tutta eternità,
Io qual Giovan Battista
　Loderò Dio:
L'Amata tanto amata
　Tuo guiderdon sarà,
E l' alma tua salvata
　Sarammi il mio.

Aprile 1867.

8

SAPESSI PURE

CHE fai lontan da me,
   Che fai, cor mio?
   Quel che facc' io
È ch' ognor penso a te.

Pensando, a te sorrido,
   Sospiro a te:
   E tu lontan da me
Tu pur sei fido?

Maggio 1867.

9

' IDDIO C' ILLUMINI

QUANDO il tempo avverrà che partiremo
   Ciascun di noi per separata via,
Momento che verrà, momento estremo
   Quando che fia:

Calcando l' uno inusitata traccia,
   Seguendo l' altro il solito suo corso,
Non ci nasca in quel dì vergogna in faccia
   Nè in sen rimorso.

Sia che tu vada pria forte soletto,
O sia ch' io ti preceda in quel sentiero,
Deh ricordiamci allor d' averci detto
Pur sempre il vero.

Quanto t' amavo e quanto! e non dovea
Esprimer quell' amor che ti portavo:
Più ma assai più di quel che non dicea
Nel cuor ti amavo.

Più di felicità, più di speranza;
Di vita non dirò, chè è poca cosa:
Dolce-amaro tu fosti in rimembranza
A me gelosa.

Ma a me tu preferisti la virtude,
La veritade, amico: e non saprai
Chi amasti alfin? Soltanto il fior si schiude
D' un sole ai rai.

Se più di me la Veritade amasti,
Gesù fu quel tuo sconosciuto Amore: —
Gesù, che sconosciuto a lui parlasti,
Vincigli il core.

Maggio 1867.

10

AMICIZIA

Sirocchia son d' Amor

VENGA Amicizia e sia la benvenuta,
   Venga, ma non perciò sen parta Amore:
Abitan l' uno e l' altra in gentil core
Che albergo ai pellegrini non rifiuta.
Ancella questa docile e compiuta,
   E quei tiranno no ma pio signore:
   Regni egli occulto nè si mostri fuore,
Essa si sveli in umiltà dovuta.
Oggi ed ancor doman per l' amicizia,
   E posdomani ancor se pur si vuole,
   Chè dolci cose apporta e non amare:
   E venga poi, ma non con luna o sole,
Giorno d' amor, giorno di gran delizia,
   Giorno che spunta non per tramontare.

Agosto 1867.

11

Luscious and sorrowful

UCCELLO delle rose e del dolore,
   Uccel d' amore,
Felice ed infelice, quel tuo canto
   È riso o pianto?
Fido all' infido, tieni in freddo lido
   Spina per nido.

Agosto 1867.

12

*O forza irresistibile
Dell' umile preghiera*

CHE Ti darò, Gesù Signor mio buono?
Ah quello ch' amo più, quello Ti dono:
Accettalo, Signor Gesù mio Dio,
Il sol mio dolce amor, anzi il cor mio;
Accettalo per Te, siati prezioso;
Accettalo per me, salva il mio sposo.
Non ho che lui, Signor, nol disprezzare,
Caro tienlo nel cor fra cose care.
Ricordati del dì che sulla croce
Pregavi Iddio così, con flebil voce,
Con anelante cor: "Questo che fanno,
Padre, perdona lor, ch' essi non sanno."
Ei pur, Signor, non sa Quello che sdegna,
Ei pure T' amerà s' uno gl' insegna.
Se tutto quanto appar, che a Te non piace,
Fugace spuma in mar, nebbia fugace;
Successo o avversità, contento o duolo,
Se tutto è vanita fuorchè Tu solo;
Se chi non prega Te nel vuoto chiama;
Se amore amor non è che Te non ama; —
Dona Te stesso a noi, ricchi saremo;
Poi nega quanto vuoi, chè tutto avremo:
Di mel più dolce Tu, che ben ci basti;
D' amore amabil più, Tu che ci amasti.

Settembre 1867.

13

FINESTRA MIA ORIENTALE

[IN MALATTIA]

VOLGO la faccia verso l' oriente,
   Verso il meriggio, ove colui dimora: —
Ben fai che vivi ai lati dell' aurora;
Chi teco vive par felice gente.
Volgo verso di te l' occhio languente,
   Lo spirito che teme e spera ancora;
   Volgiti verso quella che ti onora,
T' ama, ti brama, in core e colla mente.
Debole e stanca verso te mi volgo:
   Che sarà mai questo che sento, amico?
Ogni cara memoria tua raccolgo, —
   Quanto dirti vorrei! ma pur nol dico.
Lungi da te dei giorni me ne dolgo:
   Fossimo insieme in bel paese aprico!

     Fossimo insieme!
     Che importerebbe
       U' si facesse
       Il nostro nido?
     Cielo sarebbe
       Quasi quel lido.
       Ah fossi teco,
     Col cor ben certo

D' essere amato
Come vorrebbe!
Sì che il deserto
S' infiorirebbe.

Ottobre 1867.

14

Eppure allora venivi

O TEMPO tardo e amaro! —
Quando verrai, cor mio,
Quando, ma quando?
Siccome a me sei caro
Se cara a te foss' io,
Ti andrei cercando?

Febbrajo 1868.

15

Per Preferenza

FELICE la tua madre,
Le suore tue felici,
Che senton quanto dici,
Che vivono con te,
Che t' amano di dritto
D' amor contento e saggio:
Pur questo lor vantaggio
Non lo vorrei per me.

Quel grave aspetto tuo
Veder di quando in quando,
Frattanto andar pensando
    "Un giorno riverrà";
Ripeter nel mio core
(Qual rosa è senza spine?)
"Ei sa che l' amo alfine —
    M' ama egli ancor?"   Chi sa!

È questo assai più dolce
Dell' altro, al parer mio:
Essere in ver desio
    O tutto o nulla[1] a te;
Nè troppo vo' lagnarmi
Ch' or stai da me diviso,
Se un giorno in Paradiso
    Festeggerai con me.

Marzo 1868.

16

OGGI

POSSIBIL non sarebbe
    Ch' io non t' amassi, O Caro:
Chi mai si scorderebbe
    Del proprio core?

---

[1] Ma no; se non amante siimi amico:
    Quel ch' io sarò per te non tel predico.

Se amaro il dolce fai,
    Dolce mi fai l' amaro;
Se qualche amor mi dài,
    Ti do l' amore.

Marzo 1868.

17

TI do l' addio,
    Amico mio,
Per settimane
    Che paion lunghe:
Ti raccomando
Di quando in quando
Circoli quadri,
    Idee bislunghe.

Marzo 1868.

18

Ripetizione

CREDEA di rivederti e ancor ti aspetto;
    Di giorno in giorno ognor ti vo bramando:
Quando ti rivedrò, cor mio diletto,
    Quando ma quando?

Dissi e ridissi con perenne sete,
    E lo ridico e vo' ridirlo ancora,
Qual usignol che canta e si ripete
    Fino all' aurora.

Giugno 1868.

19

Amico e più che amico mio

COR mio a cui si volge l' altro mio core
    Qual calamita al polo, e non ti trova,
La nascita della mia vita nuova
Con pianto fu, con grida, e con dolore.
Ma l' aspro duolo fummi precursore
    Di speranza gentil che canta e cova;
    Sì, chi non prova pena amor non prova,
E quei non vive che non prova amore.
O tu che in Dio mi sei, ma dopo Iddio,
    Tutta la terra mia ed assai del cielo,
    Pensa se non m' è duol disotto a un velo
    Parlarti e non ti dir mai che ti bramo: —
Dillo tu stesso a te, dolce cor mio,
    Se pur tu m' ami dillo a te ch' io t' amo.

Agosto 1868.

20

Nostre voluntà quieti
Virtù di carità

VENTO gentil che verso il mezzodì
    Soffiando vai, deh porta un mio sospir,
Dicendo ad Un quel che non debbo dir,
Con un sospir dicendogli così:
Quella che diede un "No" volendo un "Sì"
    (Volendo e non volendo — a che ridir?),

Quella ti manda: È vanità il fiorir
Di questa vita che meniam costì.
Odi che dice e piange: È vanità
   Questo che nasce e muore amor mondan;
     Deh leva gli occhi, io gli occhi vo' levar,
  Verso il reame dove non in van
     Amasi Iddio quanto ognun possa amar
Ed il creato tutto in carità.

Agosto 1868.

21

Se così fosse

IO più ti amai che non mi amasti tu: —
  Amen, se così volle Iddio Signor;
  Amen, quantunque mi si spezzi il cor,
    Signor Gesù.

Ma Tu che Ti ricordi e tutto sai,
  Tu che moristi per virtù d'amor,
  Nell' altro mondo donami quel cor
    Che tanto amai.

Agosto 1868.

L' UOMMIBATTO

O UOMMIBATTO
   Agil, giocondo,
Che ti sei fatto
   Irsuto e tondo!
Deh non fuggire
   Qual vagabondo,
Non disparire
   Forando il mondo:
Pesa davvero
D' un emisfero
   Non lieve il pondo.
1869.

COR MIO

COR mio, cor mio,
   Più non ti veggo, ma mi rammento
Del giorno spento,
   Cor mio.
Pur ti ricordi del lungo amore,
   Cor del mio core,
      Cor mio?
Circa 1870.

ADRIANO

ANIMUCCIA, vagantuccia, morbiduccia,
    Oste del corpo e suora,
Ove or farai dimora?
Palliduccia, irrigidita, svestituccia,
    Non più scherzante or ora.
1876.

NINNA-NANNA

1

[ANGELS AT THE FOOT]

ANGELI al capo, al piede;
    E qual ricciuto agnello
Dormir fra lor si vede
Il bel mio bambinello.

2

[LOVE ME, I LOVE YOU]

    Amami, t' amo,
      Figliolin mio:
    Cantisi, suonisi,
      Con tintinnio.

Mamma t' abbraccia,
    Cor suo ti chiama;
Suonisi, cantisi,
    Ama chi t' ama.

3

[My Baby has a Father and a Mother]

E babbo e mamma ha il nostro figliolino,
    Ricco bambino.
Ma ne conosco un altro senza padre
    E senza madre —
    Il poverino!

4

[Our little Baby fell Asleep]

S' addormentò la nostra figliolina,
    Nè si risveglierà
Per giorni e giorni assai sera o mattina.
    Ma poi si sveglierà,
E con cara ridente bocchettina
    Ribacerà Mammà.
u

5

[Kookoorookoo, Kookoorookoo]

Cuccurucù — cuccurucù —
All' alba il gallo canta.
Chicchirichì — chicchirichì —
Di rose il ciel s' ammanta.
   Cuccurucù — cuccurucù —
Comincia un gorgheggiare.
Chicchirichì — chicchirichì —
Risalta il sol dal mare.

6

[Baby Cry]

Ohibò piccina
   Tutto atterrita!
La medicina
Bever si de':
Uno, due, tre,
Ed è finita.

7

[Eight o'clock]

Otto ore suonano —
Picchia il postino:
Ben cinque lettere
   Son per Papà;

Una per te,
Nulla per me;
E un bigliettino
V' è per Mammà.

8

[BREAD AND MILK FOR BREAKFAST]

Nel verno accanto al fuoco
Mangio la mia minestra,
E al pettirosso schiudo la finestra,
Ch' ei pur ne vuole un poco.

[OVVERO]

S' affaccia un pettirosso alla finestra —
Vieni vieni a gustar la mia minestra.
Lana ben foderata io porto addosso,
Ma tu non porti che un corpetto rosso.

9

[THERE'S SNOW ON THE FIELDS]

Gran freddo è infuori, e dentro è freddo un poco:
Quanto è grata una zuppa accanto al fuoco!
Mi vesto di buon panno —
Ma i poveri non hanno
Zuppa da bere e fuoco a cui sedere,
O tetto o panni in questo freddo intenso —
Ah mi si stringe il cor mentre io ci penso.

10

[I Dug and Dug amongst the Snow]

Scavai la neve — sì che scavai —
Ma fior nè foglia spuntava mai.
Scavai la rena con ansia lena,
Ma fior nè foglia spicca da rena.
O vento aprico, con fiato lieve
Sveglia i fioretti, sgela la neve!
Ma non soffiare su quella rena:
Chi soffia in rena perde la lena.

11

[Your Brother has a Falcon]

Sì che il fratello s' ha un falconcello,
   E tiene un fior la suora:
Ma che, ma che riman per te,
   Il neonato or ora?
Vo' farti cocchio del mio ginocchio,
   Minor mio figliolino:
Da capo a piè ti stringo a me,
   Minimo piccino.

12

[Hear what the mournful Linnets say]

Udite, si dolgono mesti fringuelli: —
Bel nido facemmo per cari gemelli,
Ma tre ragazzacci lo misero in stracci.
Fuggì primavera, s'imbruna la sera,
E tempo ci manca da fare un secondo
    Niduncolo tondo.

13

[A Baby's Cradle with no Baby in it]

Ahi culla vuota ed ahi sepolcro pieno
    Ove le smunte foglie autunno getta!
Lo spirto aspetta in paradiso ameno,
    Il corpo in terra aspetta.

14

[O Wind why do you never Rest?]

Lugubre e vagabondo in terra e in mare,
O vento, O vento, a che non ti posare?
Ci trai la pioggia fin dall' occidente,
E la neve ci trai dal nord fremente.

15

[O Wind where have you been?]

"Aura dolcissima, ma dondo siete?"
"Dinfra le mammole — non lo sapete?
Abbassi il viso ad adocchiar l' erbetta
Chi vuol trovar l' ascosa mammoletta.
La madreselva il dolce caldo aspetta:
Tu addolci un freddo mondo, O mammoletta."

16

[If I were a Queen]

"Foss' io regina,
  Tu re saresti:
    Davanti a te
      M' inchinerei."
"Ah foss' io re!
  Tu lo vedresti:
Si che regina
    Mi ti farei."

17

[WHAT ARE HEAVY? SEA-SAND AND SORROW]

Pesano rena e pena:
Oggi e doman son brevi:
La gioventude e un fior son cose lievi:
  Ed han profondità
Mar magno e magna verità.

18

[A TOADSTOOL COMES UP IN A NIGHT]

Basta una notte a maturare il fungo;
Un secol vuol la quercia, e non par lungo:
Anzi il secolo breve e il vesprolungo,
Chè quercia è quercia, e fungo è sempre fungo.

19

[IF A PIG WORE A WIG]

"Porco la zucca fitta in parrucca! . .
  Che gli diresti mai?"
"M' inchinerei, l' ossequierei —
  'Ser Porco, come stai?'"
"Ahi guai per caso mai
Se la coda andasse a male?" . . .
"Sta tranquillo — buon legale
Gli farebbe un codicillo."

20

[Hopping Frog, hop here and be seen]

Salta, ranocchio, e mostrati;
Non celo pietra in mano:
Merletto in testa e verde vesta,
Vattene salvo e sano.
Rospo lordo, deh non celarti:
Tutto il mondo può disprezzarti,
Ma mal non fai nè mal vo' farti.

21

[Where innocent bright-eyed Daisies are]

Spunta la margherita
  Qual astro in sullo stelo,
E l' erbetta infiorita
  Rassembra un verde cielo.

22

[A motherless soft Lambkin]

Agnellina orfanellina
Giace in cima alla collina,
Fredda, sola, senza madre,
  Senza madre ohime!
Io sarotti e madre e padre,
Io sarò tua pastorella;
Non tremar, diletta agnella,
  Io ci penso a te.

23

[When Fishes set Umbrellas up]

Amico pesce, piover vorrà;
Prendi l' ombrello se vuoi star secco.
Ed ecco!
Domani senza fallo si vedrà
Lucertolon zerbino
Ripararsi dal sol coll' ombrellino.

24

[A Ring upon her Finger]

Sposa velata,
Inanellata,
Mite e sommessa:
Sposo rapito,
Insuperbito,
Accanto ad essa.
Amici, amori,
Cantando a coro,
Davanti a loro
Spargete fiori.

25

[THE HORSES OF THE SEA]

 Cavalli marittimi
  Urtansi in guerra,
 E meglio ci servono
  Quelli di terra.
 Questi pacifici
  Corrono o stanno;
 Quei rotolandosi
  Spumando vanno.

26

[O SAILOR, COME ASHORE]

"O marinaro, che mi apporti tu?"
"Coralli rossi e bianchi tratti in su
  Dal mar profondo.
Pianti non son nè si scavar da mina:
Minime creature in salsa brina
  Fecerne mondo."

27

[THE ROSE WITH SUCH A BONNY BLUSH]

 Arrossice la rosa — e perchè mai?
 A cagione del sol: ma, sol, che fai?
  E tu, rosa, che t' hai
 Che ti fai rosea sì se bene stai?

28

[THE ROSE THAT BLUSHES ROSY RED]

La rosa china il volto rosseggiato,
  E bene fà:
Il giglio innalza il viso immacolato,
  E ben gli stà.

29

[OH FAIR TO SEE]

O ciliegia infiorita,
La bianco-rivestita,
 Bella sei tu.
O ciliegia infruttata,
La verde-inghirlandata,
La rosso-incoronata,
 Bella sei tu.

30

[GOOD-BYE IN FEAR, GOOD-BYE IN SORROW]

"In tema e in pena addio,
 Addio ma in van, tu sai;
Per sempre addio, cor mio."
 "E poi più mai."
"Oggi e domani addio,
 Nel secolo de' guai
A tutto tempo addio."
 "E poi più·mai."

31

[BABY LIES SO FAST ASLEEP]

D' un sonno profondissimo
  Dorme la suora mia:
Gli angeli bianchi aligeri
  Verranno a trarla via?
In sonno profondissimo
  Calma e contenta giace:
Un fiore in man lasciamole,
  Un bacio in fronte — e pace.

32

[LULLABY OH LULLABY]

Ninna-nanna, ninna-nanna,
  Giace e dorme l' agnellina.
Ninna-nanna, ninna-nanna,
  Monna Luna s' incammina.
Ninna-nanna, ninna-nanna,
  Tace e dorme l' uccellino.
Ninna-nanna, ninna-nanna,
  Dormi, dormi, o figliolino.
Ninna-nanna, ninna-nanna.

33

[LIE A-BED]

Capo che chinasi,
Occhi che chiudonsi —
A letto, a letto,
Sonnacchiosetto!
Dormi, carino,
Fino al mattino, —
Dormi, carino.

Circa 1879.

SOGNANDO

Ne' sogni ti veggo,
 . Amante ed amico;
Ai piedi ti seggo,
 Ti tengo tuttor.
Nè chiedi nè chieggo,
 Nè dici nè dico,
 L' amore ab antico
  Che scaldaci il cor.
Ah voce se avessi
 Me stessa a scoprire —
Ah esprimer sapessi
  L' angoscia e l' amor!
Ah almen se potessi
 A lungo dormire,
  Nè pianger nè dire,
  Mirandoti ognor!

Circa 1890.

JUVENILIA

TO MY MOTHER

On the Anniversary of her Birth

(Presented with a Nosegay)

TO-DAY'S your natal day;
    Sweet flowers I bring:
Mother, accept I pray
    My offering.

And may you happy live,
    And long us bless;
Receiving as you give
    Great happiness.

27 April 1842.

HYMN

TO the God who reigns on high,
    To the Eternal Majesty,
To the Blessed Trinity,
Glory on earth be given,
In the sea and in the sky,
And in the highest heaven.

2 July 1843.
    x

LOVE AND HOPE

LOVE for ever dwells in heaven, —
    Hope entereth not there.
To despairing man Love's given, —
    Hope dwells not with despair.
Love reigneth high, and reigneth low, and reigneth everywhere.

In the inmost heart Love dwelleth, —
    It may not quenchèd be;
E'en when the life blood welleth,
    Its fond effects we see
In the name that leaves the lips the last — fades last from memory.

And when we shall awaken,
    Ascending to the sky,
Though Hope shall have forsaken,
    Sweet Love shall never die:
For perfect Love and perfect bliss shall be our lot on high.

9 *October* 1843.

ON ALBINA

THE roses lingered in her cheeks
    When fair Albina fainted;
O gentle reader, could it be
    That fair Albina painted?

June 1844.

FORGET ME NOT

"Forget me not, forget me not!"
   The maiden once did say,
When to some far-off battlefield
   Her lover sped away.

"Forget me not, forget me not!"
   Says now the chamber-maid,
When the traveller on his journey
   No more will be delayed.

19 *August* 1844.

CHARITY

I praised the myrtle and the rose,
   At sunrise in their beauty lying:
I passed them at the short day's close,
   And both were dying.

The summer sun his rays was throwing
   Brightly: yet ere I sought my rest
His last cold ray, more deeply glowing,
   Died in the west.

After this bleak world's stormy weather,
All, all, save Love alone, shall die;
For Faith and Hope shall merge together
In Charity.

20 *September* 1844.

(The foregoing verses are imitated from that beautiful little poem *Virtue*, by George Herbert.)

EARTH AND HEAVEN

WATER calmly flowing,
   Sunlight deeply glowing,
Swans some river riding
That is gently gliding
By the fresh green rushes,
The sweet rose that blushes,
Hyacinths whose dower
Is both scent and flower,
Skylark's soaring motion,
Sunrise from the ocean,
Jewels that lie sparkling
'Neath the waters darkling,
Seaweed, coral, amber,
Flowers that climb and clamber
Or more lowly flourish
Where the earth may nourish:
All these are beautiful,
Of beauty earth is full:

Say, to our promised heaven
Can greater charms be given?
Yes, for aye in heaven doth dwell,
Glowing, indestructible,
What here below finds tainted birth
In the corrupted sons of earth:
For, filling there and satisfying
Man's soul unchanging and undying,
Earth's fleeting joys and beauties far above,
In heaven is Love.

28 *December* 1844.

LOVE EPHEMERAL

LOVE is sweet, and so are flowers
  Blooming in bright summer bowers;
So are waters, clear and pure,
In some hidden fountain's store;
So is the soft southern breeze
Sighing low among the trees;
So is the bright queen of heaven
Reigning in the quiet even.
Yet the pallid moon may breed
Madness in man's feeble seed;
And the wind's soft influence
Often breathes the pestilence;

And the waves may sullied be
As they hurry to the sea;
Flowers soon must fade away:
Love endures but for a day.

25 *February* 1845.

BURIAL ANTHEM

FLESH of our flesh, bone of our bone —
For thou and we in Christ are one —
Thy soul unto its rest hath flown
And thou hast left us all alone
    Our weary race to run
In doubt and want and sin and pain,
Whilst thou wilt never sin again.
For us remaineth heaviness;
Thou never more shalt feel distress, —
    For thou hast found repose
Beside the bright eternal river,
That clear and pure flows on for ever
    And sings as on it flows.
And it is better far for thee
    To reach at once thy rest
Than share with us earth's misery
    Or tainted joy at best.
Brother, we will not mourn for thee,
    Although our hearts be weary

Of struggling with our enemy
    When all around is dreary:
But we will pray that still we may
Press onward in the narrow way,
With a calm thankful resignation,
And joy in this our desolation;
And we will hope at length to be
With our Great Head — and, friend, with thee —
    Beside that river blest.

3 *March* 1845.

SUMMER

HARK to the song of greeting! The tall trees
    Murmur their welcome in the southern breeze;
Amid the thickest foliage many a bird
Sits singing, their shrill matins scarcely heard
    One by one, but all together
    Welcoming the sunny weather;
    In every bower hums a bee
    Fluttering melodiously:
    Murmurs joy in every brook,
    Rippling with a pleasant look:
What greet they with their guileless bliss?
What welcome with a song like this?

    See in the south a radiant form,
        Her fair head crowned with roses;

SUMMER

From her bright footpath flies the storm;
    Upon her breast reposes
Many an unconfinèd tress,
Golden, glossy, motionless.
Face and form are love and light,
Soft ineffably, yet bright.
All her path is strewn with flowers;
Round her float the laughing Hours;
Heaven and Earth make joyful din,
Welcoming sweet Summer in.

    And now she alights on the earth
        To play with her children the flowers;
She touches the stems, and the buds have birth,
        And gently she trains them in bowers.
    And the bees and the birds are glad,
        And the wind catches warmth from her breath,
    And around her is nothing sad
        Nor any traces of death.
See now she lays her down
With roses for her crown,
With jessamine and myrtle
Forming her fragrant kirtle.
Conquered by softest slumbers,
No more the hours she numbers —
The hours that intervene
    Ere she may wing her flight
Far from this smiling scene
    With all her love and light,

And leave the flowers and the summer bowers
To wither in autumn and winter hours.

   And must they wither then?
     Their life and their perfume
   Sinking so soon again
     Into their earthy tomb.
Let us bind her as she lies
Ere the fleeting moment flies,
Hand and foot and arm and bosom,
With a chain of bud and blossom;
Twine red roses round her hands;
Round her feet twine myrtle bands.
Heap up flowers, higher, higher, —
Tulips like a glowing fire,
Clematis of milky whiteness,
Sweet geraniums' varied brightness,
Honeysuckle, commeline,
Roses, myrtles, jessamine;
Heap them higher, bloom on bloom,
Bury her as in a tomb.

   But alas they are withered all,
     And how can dead flowers bind her?
   She pushes away her pall,
     And she leaves the dead behind her:
   And she flies across the seas,
     To gladden for a time
   The blossoms and the bees
     Of some far-distant clime.

4 *December* 1845.

SERENADE

COME, wander forth with me: the orange flowers
Breathe faintest perfume from the summer bowers.
Come, wander forth with me; the moon on high
Shines proudly in a flood of brilliancy;
    Around her car each burning star
    Gleams like a beacon from afar.
The night wind scarce disturbs the sea
As it sighs forth so languidly,
Laden with sweetness like a bee;
And all is still, below, above,
Save murmurs of the turtle-dove
That murmurs ever of its love.
For now 'tis the hour, the balmy hour,
When the strains of love have chiefly power;
When the maid looks forth from her latticed bower,
With a gentle yielding smile,
Donning her mantle all the while.
Now the moon beams down on high
From her halo brilliantly,
By the dark clouds unencumbered
That once o'er her pale face slumbered:
Far from her mild rays flutters Folly,
For on them floats calm Melancholy; —
A passionless sadness without dread,
Like the thought of those we love, long dead;

Full of hope and chastened joy,
Heavenly, without earth's alloy.
Listen, dearest: all is quiet —
Slumbering the world's toil and riot;
And all is fair in earth and sky and sea.
Come, wander forth with me.

4 *December* 1845.

THE END OF TIME

THOU who art dreary
　With a cureless woe,
Thou who art weary
Of all things below,
Thou who art weeping
By the loved sick bed,
Thou who art keeping
Watches o'er the dead, —
Hope, hope! old Time flies fast upon his way,
And soon will cease the night, and soon will dawn
the day.

The rose blooms brightly,
But it fades ere night;
And youth flies lightly,
Yet how sure its flight!
And still the river
Merges in the sea;

THE END OF TIME

And Death reigns ever
Whilst old Time shall be; —
Yet hope! old Time flies fast upon his way,
And soon will cease the night, and soon will dawn
the day.

All we most cherish
In this world below,
What though it perish?
It has aye been so.
So through all ages
It has ever been,
To fools and sages,
Noble men and mean: —
Yet hope, still hope! for Time flies on his way,
And soon will end the night, and soon will dawn
the day.

All of each nation
Shall that morning see
With exultation
Or with misery:
From watery slumbers,
From the opening sod,
Shall rise up numbers
To be judged by God.
Then hope and fear, for Time speeds on his way,
And soon must end the night, and soon must dawn
the day.

9 *December* 1845.

AMORE E DOVERE

CHIAMI il mio core
 Crudele, altero:
No non è vero,
 Crudel non è:
T' amo, t' amai —
E tu lo sai —
Men del dovere,
 Ma più di me.

O ruscelletto,
 Dì al Dio d' Amore
Che questo petto,
 Che questo core,
A lui ricetto
 Più non darà.
L' alme tradisce
 Senza rimorso;
Non compatisce,
 Non dà soccorso,
E si nudrisce
 Di crudeltà. —

T' intendo, ti lagni,
Mio povero core;
T' intendo, l' Amore
 Si lagna di me.

Deh placati alfine!
Mi pungon le spine
Che vengon da te.

1845 *to* 1847.

MOTHER AND CHILD

"What art thou thinking of," said the mother,
   "What art thou thinking of, my child?"
"I was thinking of heaven," he answered her,
   And looked up in her face and smiled.

"And what didst thou think of heaven?" she said;
   "Tell me, my little one."
"Oh I thought that there the flowers never fade,
   That there never sets the sun."

"And wouldst thou love to go thither, my child,
   Thither wouldst thou love to go,
And leave the pretty flowers that wither,
   And the sun that sets below?"

"Oh I would be glad to go there, mother,
   To go and live there now;
And I would pray for thy coming, mother; —
   My mother, wouldst not thou?"

10 *January* 1846.

ON THE DEATH OF A CAT

A FRIEND OF MINE AGED TEN YEARS AND A HALF

WHO shall tell the lady's grief
    When her Cat was past relief?
Who shall number the hot tears
Shed o'er her, belov'd for years?
Who shall say the dark dismay
Which her dying caused that day?

Come, ye Muses, one and all,
Come obedient to my call;
Come and mourn with tuneful breath
Each one for a separate death;
And, while you in numbers sigh,
I will sing her elegy.

Of a noble race she came,
And Grimalkin was her name.
Young and old full many a mouse
Felt the prowess of her house;
Weak and strong full many a rat
Cowered beneath her crushing pat;
And the birds around the place
Shrank from her too close embrace.
But one night, reft of her strength,
She lay down and died at length:

Lay a kitten by her side
In whose life the mother died.
Spare her line and lineage,
Guard her kitten's tender age,
And that kitten's name as wide
Shall be known as hers that died.
And whoever passes by
The poor grave where Puss doth lie,
Softly, softly let him tread,
Nor disturb her narrow bed.

14 *March* 1846.

LOVE ATTACKED

LOVE is more sweet than flowers,
   But sooner dying;
Warmer than sunny hours,
   But faster flying;

Softer than music whispers,
   Springing with day,
To murmur till the vespers,
   Then die away;

More kind than friendship's greeting,
   But as untrue;
Brighter than hope, but fleeting
   More swiftly too.

LOVE ATTACKED

Like breath of summer breezes
   Gently it sighs,
But soon alas one ceases,
   The other dies:

And like an inundation
   It leaves behind .
An utter desolation
   Of heart and mind.

Who then would court Love's presence,
   If here below
It can but be the essence
   Of restless woe?

Returned or unrequited,
   'Tis still the same;
The flame was never lighted,
   Or sinks the flame.

Yet all, both fools and sages,
   Have felt its power,
In distant lands and ages,—
   Here, at this hour.

Then what from fear and weeping
   Shall give me rest?
Oh tell me, ye who sleeping
   At length are blest!

In answer to my crying,
　　Sounds like incense
Rose from the earth, replying,
　　"Indifference."

21 *April* 1846.

LOVE DEFENDED

WHO extols a wilderness?
　　Who hath praised indifference?
Foolish one, thy words are sweet,
　　But devoid of sense.

As the man who ne'er hath seen,
Or as he who cannot hear,
Is the heart that hath no part
　　In Love's hope and fear.

True, the blind do not perceive
The unsightly things around;
True, the deaf man trembleth not
　　At an awful sound.

But the face of heaven and earth,
And the murmur of the main,
Surely are a recompense
　　For a little pain.

So, though Love may not be free
Always from a taint of grief,
If its sting is very sharp,
  Great is its relief.

23 April 1846.

THE MARTYR

SEE, the sun hath risen —
  Lead her from the prison;
She is young and tender, — lead her tenderly:
  May no fear subdue her,
  Lest the saints be fewer —
Lest her place in heaven be lost eternally.

  Forth she came, not trembling,
  No nor yet dissembling
An o'erwhelming terror weighing her down, down;
  Little, little heeding
  Earth, but inly pleading
For the strength to triumph and to win a crown.

  All her might was rallied
  To her heart; not pallid
Was her cheek, but glowing with a glorious red;
  Glorious red and saintly,
  Never paling faintly,
But still flushing, kindling still, without thought of
    dread.

On she went, on faster,
Trusting in her Master,
Feeling that His eye watched o'er her lovingly;
He would prove and try her,
But would not deny her
When her soul had past, for His sake, patiently.

"Christ," she said, "receive me, —
Let no terrors grieve me, —
Take my soul and guard it with Thy heavenly cares:
Take my soul and guard it, —
Take it and reward it
With the love Thou bearest for the love it bears."

Quickened with a fire
Of sublime desire,
She looked up to heaven, and she cried aloud:
"Death, I do entreat thee,
Come! I go to meet thee;
Wrap me in the whiteness of a virgin shroud."

On she went, hope-laden —
Happy, happy maiden!
Never more to tremble, and to weep no more:
All her sins forgiven,
Straight the path to heaven,
Through the glowing fire, lay her feet before.

On she went, on quickly,
And her breath came thickly,

With the longing to see God coming pantingly:
    Now the fire is kindled,
    And her flesh has dwindled
Unto dust; — her soul is mounting up on high:

    Higher, higher mounting,
    The swift moments counting, —
Fear is left beneath her, and the chastening rod:
    Tears no more shall blind her;
    Trouble lies behind her;
Satisfied with hopeful rest, and replete with God.

24 *May* 1846.

THE DYING MAN TO HIS BETROTHED

ONE word — 'tis all I ask of thee;
    One word — and that is little now
That I have learned thy wrong of me;
    And thou too art unfaithful — thou!
O thou sweet poison, sweetest death,
O honey between serpent's teeth,
Breathe on me with thy scorching breath!

The last poor hope is fleeting now,
    And with it life is ebbing fast;
I gaze upon thy cold white brow,
    And loathe and love thee to the last.

And still thou keepest silence, — still
Thou look'st on me: for good or ill
Speak out, that I may know thy will.

Thou weepest, woman, and art pale:
 Weep not, for thou shalt soon be free;
My life is ending like a tale
 That was but never more shall be.
O blessed moments, ye fleet fast,
And soon the latest shall be past,
And she will be content at last.

Nay, tremble not, I have not curst
 Thy house or mine, or thee or me.
The moment that I saw thee first,
 The moment that I first loved thee, —
Curse *them?* — Alas I can but bless
In this mine hour of heaviness: —
Nay, sob not so in thy distress.

I have been harsh, thou say'st of me; —
 God knows my heart was never so;
It never could be so to thee.
 And now it is too late — I know
Thy grief — forgive me, love, 'tis o'er;
For I shall never trouble more
Thy life that was so calm before.

I pardon thee; mayst thou be blest!
 Say, wilt thou sometimes think of me?

Oh may I, from my happy rest,
   Still look with love on thine and thee, —
And may I pray for thee alway,
And for thy love still may I pray,
Waiting the everlasting day!

Stoop over me; — ah this is death!
   I scarce can see thee at my side:
Stoop lower; let me feel thy breath,
   O thou, mine own, my promised bride!
Pardon me, love; — I pardon thee:
And may our pardon sealèd be
Throughout the long eternity.

The pains of death my senses cover.
   Oh for His sake who died for men,
Be thou more true to this thy lover
   Than thou hast been to me: Amen.
And, if he chide thee wrongfully,
One little moment think on me,
And thou wilt bear it patiently.

And now, O God, I turn to Thee:
   Thou only, Father, canst not fail:
Lord, Thou hast tried and broken me,
   And yet Thy mercy shall prevail.
Saviour, through Thee I am forgiven; —
Do Thou receive my soul, blood-shriven,
O Christ, who art the Gate of Heaven!

14 *July* 1846.

LISETTA ALL' AMANTE

PERDONA al primo eccesso
 D' un tenero dolore;
A te promisi il core,
 E vo' serbarlo a te.
Ma dimmi e mi consola:
M' ami tu ancor, cor mio?
Se a te fedel son io,
 Sarai fedele a me?

Chè se nell' alma ingrata
Pensi ad abbandonarmi,
Anch' io saprò scordarmi
 D' un amator crudel.
Ma crederlo non voglio,
Ma non lo vo' pensare;
Chè nol potrei lasciare,
 Chè gli sarei fedel.

Folkestone, 11 *August* 1846.

THE DEAD BRIDE

THERE she lay so still and pale,
    With her bridal robes around her:
Joy is fleeting, life is frail,
    Death had found her.

Gone for ever: gone away
    From the love and light of earth;
Gone for ever: who shall say
    Where her second birth?

Had her life been good and kind?
    Had her heart been meek and pure?
Was she of a lowly mind,
    Ready to endure?

Did she still console the sad,
    Soothe the widow's anguish wild,
Make the poor and needy glad,
    Tend the orphan child?

Who shall say what hope and fear
    Crowded in her short life's span?
If the love of God was dear
    Or the love of man?

THE DEAD BRIDE

Happy bride if single-hearted
   Her first love to God was given;
If from this world she departed
   But to dwell in heaven;

If her faith on heaven was fixed
   And her hope; if charity
Filled her full of light unmixed
   With earth's vanity.

But alas, if tainted pleasure
   Won her heart and held it here,
Where is now her failing treasure,
   All her gladness where? . . .

Hush, too curious questioner;
   Hush, and think thine own sins o'er.
Little canst thou learn from her;
   For we know no more

Than that there she lies all pale
   With her bridal robes around her:
Joy is fleeting — life is frail —
   Death hath found her.

Folkestone, 10 *September* 1846.

WILL THESE HANDS NE'ER BE CLEAN?

AND who is this lies prostrate at thy feet?
And is he dead, thou man of wrath and pride?
Yes, now thy vengeance is complete,
    Thy hate is satisfied.
What had he done to merit this of thee?
Who gave thee power to take away his life?
O deeply-rooted direful enmity
    That ended in long strife!
See where he grasped thy mantle as he fell,
Staining it with his blood; how terrible
Must be the payment due for this in hell!

And dost thou think to go and see no more
Thy bleeding victim, now the struggle's o'er?
  To find out peace in other lands,
  And wash the red mark from thy hands?
  It shall not be; for everywhere
  He shall be with thee; and the air
  Shall smell of blood, and on the wind
  His groans pursue thee close behind.
  When waking he shall stand before thee;
And when at length sleep shall come o'er thee,
  Powerless to move, alive to dream,
  So dreadful shall thy visions seem
  That thou shalt own them even to be
  More hateful than reality.

WILL THESE HANDS NE'ER BE CLEAN?

What time thou stoopest down to drink
Of limpid waters, thou shalt think
It is thy foe's blood bubbles up
From the polluted fountain's cup,
That stains thy lip, that cries to heaven
For vengeance — and it shall be given.

And when thy friends shall question thee,
"Why art thou changed so heavily?"
Trembling and fearful shalt thou say
"I am not changed," and turn away;
For such an outcast thou shalt be
Thou wilt not dare ask sympathy.

And so thy life will pass, and day by day
The current of existence flow away;
And, though to thee earth shall be hell and breath
Vengeance, yet thou shalt tremble more at death.
And one by one thy friends will learn to fear thee,
And thou shalt live without a hope to cheer thee;
Lonely amid a thousand, chained though free,
The curse of memory shall cling to thee:
Ages may pass away, worlds rise and set —
    But thou shalt not forget.

Folkestone, 16 *September* 1846.

PRESENT AND FUTURE

WHAT is life that we should love it,
    Cherishing it evermore,
Never prizing aught above it,
    Ever loth to give it o'er?
Is it goodness? is it gladness?
Nay, 'tis more of sin and sadness,
    Nay, of weariness 'tis more.

Earthly joys are very fleeting,
    Earthly sorrows very long;
Parting ever follows meeting,
    Night succeeds to evensong.
Storms may darken in the morning
And eclipse the sun's bright dawning,
    And the chilly gloom prolong.

But, though clouds may screen and hide it,
    The sun shines for evermore.
Then bear grief in hope: abide it
    Knowing that it must give o'er:
And the darkness shall flee from us,
And the sun beam down upon us
    Ever glowing more and more.

5 *November* 1846.

THE TIME OF WAITING

LIFE is fleeting, joy is fleeting,
Coldness follows love and greeting,
Parting still succeeds to meeting.

If I say, "Rejoice to-day,"
Sorrow meets me in the way:
I cannot my will obey.

If I say, "My grief shall cease;
Now then I will live in peace":
My cares instantly increase.

When I look up to the sky,
Thinking to see light on high,
Clouds my searching glance defy.

When I look upon the earth
For the flowers that should have birth,
I find dreariness and dearth.

And the winds sigh on for ever,
Murmurs still the flowing river,
On the graves the sunbeams quiver.

And destruction waxeth bold,
And the earth is growing old,
And I tremble in the cold.

And my weariness increases
To an ache that never ceases
And a pain that ne'er decreases.

And the times are turbulent,
And the Holy Church is rent,
And who tremble or repent?

And loud cries do ever rise
To the portals of the skies
From our earthly miseries;

From love slighted, not requited;
From high hope that should have lighted
All our path up, now benighted;

From the woes of humankind;
From the darkness of the mind;
From all anguish undefined;

From the heart that's crushed and sinking;
From the brain grown blank with thinking;
From the spirit sorrow drinking.

All cry out with pleading strong:
"Vengeance, Lord! how long, how long
Shall we suffer this great wrong?"

And the pleading and the cry
Of earth's sons are heard on high,
And are noted verily.

THE TIME OF WAITING

When this world shall be no more,
The oppressors shall endure
The great vengeance which is sure.

And the sinful shall remain
To an endless death and pain;
But the good shall live again, —

Never more to be oppressed;
Balm shall heal the bleeding breast,
And the weary be at rest.

All shall vanish of dejection,
Grief and fear and imperfection,
In that glorious resurrection.

Heed not then a night of sorrow,
If the dawning of the morrow
From past grief fresh beams shall borrow.

Thankful for whate'er is given,
Strive we, as we ne'er have striven,
For love's sake to be forgiven.

Then, the dark clouds opening,
Even to us the sun shall bring
Gladness, and sweet flowers shall spring.

For Christ's guiding love alway,
For the everlasting day,
For meek patience, let us pray.

16 *November* 1846.

TASSO AND LEONORA

A GLORIOUS vision hovers o'er his soul,
  Gilding the prison and the weary bed, —
Though hard the pillow placed beneath his head,
Though brackish be the water in the bowl
  Beside him; he can see the planets roll
In glowing adoration, without dread;
Knowing how, by unerring wisdom led,
They struggle not against the strong control.
  When suddenly a star shoots from the skies,
Than all the other stars more purely bright,
Replete with heavenly loves and harmonies;
  He starts: — what meets his full awakening sight?
Lo! Leonora, with large humid eyes,
Gazing upon him in the misty light.

19 *December* 1846.

THE SOLITARY ROSE

O HAPPY rose, red rose, that bloomest lonely
    Where there are none to gather while they
      love thee;
That art perfumed by thine own fragrance only,
  Resting like incense round thee and above thee; —
Thou hearest nought save some pure stream that
      flows,
    O happy rose.
z

What though for thee no nightingales are singing?
  They chant one eve, but hush them in the morning.
Near thee no little moths and bees are winging
  To steal thy honey when the day is dawning; —
Thou keep'st thy sweetness till the twilight's close,
    O happy rose.

Then rest in peace, thou lone and lovely flower;
  Yea be thou glad, knowing that none are near thee,
To mar thy beauty in a wanton hour,
  And scatter all thy leaves nor deign to wear thee.
Securely in thy solitude repose,
    O happy rose.

15 *March* 1847.

THE SONG OF THE STAR

I AM a Star dwelling on high
In the azure of the vaulted sky.
I shine on the land and I shine on the sea,
And the little breezes talk to me.
The waves rise towards me every one,
And forget the brightness of the sun:
The growing grass springs up towards me,
And forgets the day's fertility.
My face is light, and my beam is life,
And my passionless being hath no strife.
In me no love is turned to hate,

No fullness is made desolate;
Here is no hope, no fear, no grief,
Here is no pain and no relief;
Nor birth nor death hath part in me,
But a profound tranquillity.
The blossoms that bloomed yesterday
Unaltered shall bloom on to-day,
And on the morrow shall not fade.
Within the everlasting shade
The fountain gushing up for ever
Flows on to the eternal river,
That, running by a reedy shore,
Bubbles, bubbles evermore.
The happy birds sing in the trees
To the music of the southern breeze;
And they fear no lack of food,
Chirping in the underwood;
For ripe seeds and berried bushes
Serve the finches and the thrushes,
And all feathered fowls that dwell
In that shade majestical.
Beyond all clouds and all mistiness
I float in the strength of my loveliness.
And I move round the sun with a measured motion
In the blue expanse of the skyey ocean;
And I hear the song of the angel throng
In a river of extasy flow along,
Without a pausing, without a hushing,
Like an everlasting fountain's gushing
That of its own will bubbles up

From a white untainted cup.
Countless planets float round me,
Differing all in majesty;
Smaller some, and some more great,
Amethystine, roseate,
Golden, silvery, glowing blue,
Hueless, and of every hue.
Each and all, both great and small,
With a cadence musical,
Shoot out rays of glowing praise
Never ending, but always
Hymning the Creator's might
Who hath filled them full of light,
Pealing through eternity,
Filling out immensity;
Sun and moon and stars together
In heights where is no cloudy weather;
Where is nor storm nor mist nor rain,
Where night goeth not to come again.
On and on and on for ever,
Never ceasing, sinking never,
Voiceless adorations rise
To the heaven above the skies.
We all chant with a holy harmony,
No discord marreth our melody;
Here are no strifes nor envyings,
But each with love joyously sings,
For ever and ever floating free
In the azure light of infinity.

19 *March* 1847.

RESURRECTION EVE

HE resteth: weep not;
　　The living sleep not
With so much calm.
　He hears no chiding
　And no deriding,
　Hath joy for sorrow,
　For night hath morrow,
For wounds hath balm,
For life's strange riot
Hath death and quiet.
Who would recall him
　Of those that love him?
No fears appall him,
No ills befall him;
　There's nought above him
Save turf and flowers
　And pleasant grass.
Pass the swift hours,
　How swiftly pass!
The hours of slumber
He doth not number;
Grey hours of morning
Ere the day's dawning;
Brightened by gleams
Of the sunbeams, —
By the foreseeing

Of resurrection,
Of glorious being,
Of full perfection,
Of sins forgiven
Before the face
Of men and spirits;
Of God in heaven,
The resting-place
That he inherits.

8 *April* 1847.

THE DEAD CITY

ONCE I rambled in a wood
With a careless hardihood,
Heeding not the tangled way;
Labyrinths around me lay,
But for them I never stood.

On, still on, I wandered on,
And the sun above me shone;
And the birds around me winging
With their everlasting singing
Made me feel not quite alone.

In the branches of the trees
Murmured like the hum of bees
The low sound of happy breezes,
Whose sweet voice that never ceases
Lulls the heart to perfect ease.

Streamlets bubbled all around
On the green and fertile ground,
   Through the rushes and the grass,
   Like a sheet of liquid glass,
With a soft and trickling sound.

And I went, I went on faster,
Contemplating no disaster;
   And I plucked ripe blackberries,
   But the birds with envious eyes·
Came and stole them from their master.

For the birds here were all tame;
Some with bodies like a flame;
   Some that glanced the branches through,
   Pure and colourless as dew;
Fearlessly to me they came.

Before me no mortal stood
In the mazes of that wood;
   Before me the birds had never
   Seen a man, but dwelt for ever
In a happy solitude:

Happy solitude, and blest
With beatitude of rest;
   Where the woods are ever vernal,
   And the life and joy eternal,
Without death's or sorrow's test.

O most blessed solitude!
O most full beatitude!
　　Where are quiet without strife
　　And imperishable life,
·Nothing marred and all things good.

And the bright sun, life-begetting,
Never rising, never setting,
　　Shining warmly overhead,
　　Nor too pallid nor too red,
Lulled me to a sweet forgetting —

Sweet forgetting of the time;
And I listened for no chime
　　Which might warn me to be gone;
　　But I wandered on, still on,
'Neath the boughs of oak and lime.

Know I not how long I strayed
In the pleasant leafy shade;
　　But the trees had gradually
　　Grown more rare, the air more free,
The sun hotter overhead.

Soon the birds no more were seen
Glancing through the living green,
　　And a blight had passed upon
　　All the trees, and the pale sun
Shone with a strange lurid sheen.

Then a darkness spread around:
I saw nought; I heard no sound:
  Solid darkness overhead,
  With a trembling cautious tread
Passed I o'er the unseen ground.

But at length a pallid light
Broke upon my searching sight;
  A pale solitary ray.
  Like a star at dawn of day
Ere the sun is hot and bright.

Towards its faintly glimmering beam
I went on as in a dream —
  A strange dream of hope and fear —
  And I saw, as I drew near,
'Twas in truth no planet's gleam;

But a lamp above a gate
Shone in solitary state,
  O'er a desert drear and cold,
  O'er a heap of ruins old,
O'er a scene most desolate.

By that gate I entered lone
A fair city of white stone;
  And a lovely light to see
  Dawned, and spread most gradually,
Till the air grew warm and shone.

Through the splendid streets I strayed
In that radiance without shade;
  Yet I heard no human sound;
  All was still and silent round
As a city of the dead.

All the doors were open wide;
Lattices on every side
  In the wind swung to and fro —
  Wind that whispered very low,
"Go and see the end of pride."

With a fixed determination
Entered I each habitation;
  But they all were tenantless.
  All was utter loneliness,
All was deathless desolation.

In the noiseless market-place
Was no careworn busy face;
  There were none to buy or sell,
  None to listen or to tell,
In this silent emptiness.

Through the city on I went
Full of awe and wonderment.
  Still the light around me shone,
  And I wandered on, still on,
In my great astonishment.

Till at length I reached a place
Where amid an ample space
   Rose a palace for a king;
   Golden was the turreting,
And of solid gold the base.

The great porch was ivory,
And the steps were ebony;
   Diamond and chrysoprase
   Set the pillars in a blaze,
Capitalled with jewelry.

None was there to bar my way,
And the breezes seemed to say,
   "Touch not these, but pass them by,
   Pressing onwards"; therefore I
Entered in and made no stay.

All around was desolate.
I went on; a silent state
   Reigned in each deserted room,
   And I hastened through the gloom
Till I reached an outer gate.

Soon a shady avenue,
Blossom-perfumed, met my view;
   Here and there the sunbeams fell
   On pure founts whose sudden swell
Up from marble basons flew.

THE DEAD CITY

Every tree was fresh and green;
Not a withered leaf was seen
   Through the veil of flowers and fruit;
   Strong and sapful were the root,
The top boughs, and all between.

Vines were climbing everywhere,
Full of purple grapes and fair.
   And far off I saw the corn
   With its heavy head down borne
By the odour-laden air.

Who shall strip the bending vine?
Who shall tread the press for wine?
   Who shall bring the harvest in
   When the pallid ears begin
In the sun to glow and shine?

On I went alone, alone,
Till I saw a tent that shone
   With each bright and lustrous hue;
   It was trimmed with jewels too,
And with flowers; not one was gone.

Then the breezes whispered me:
"Enter in, and look, and see
   How for luxury and pride
   A great multitude have died."
And I entered tremblingly.

THE DEAD CITY

Lo a splendid banquet laid
In the cool and pleasant shade.
  Mighty tables everything
  Of sweet Nature's furnishing
That was rich and rare displayed;

And each strange and luscious cate
Practised art makes delicate;
  With a thousand fair devices
  Full of odours and of spices;
And a warm voluptuous state.

All the vessels were of gold,
Set with gems of worth untold.
  In the midst a fountain rose
  Of pure milk, whose rippling flows
In a silver bason rolled.

In green emerald baskets were
  Sun-red apples, streaked and fair;
  Here the nectarine and peach
And ripe plum lay, and on each
The bloom rested everywhere.

Grapes were hanging overhead,
Purple, pale, and ruby-red;
  · And in panniers all around
  Yellow melons shone, fresh found,
With the dew upon them spread.

And the apricot and pear
And the pulpy fig were there,
   Cherries and dark mulberries,
   Bunchy currants, strawberries,
And the lemon wan and fair:

And unnumbered others too,
Fruits of every size and hue,
   Juicy in their ripe perfection,
   Cool beneath the cool reflection
Of the curtains' skyey blue.

All the floor was strewn with flowers
Fresh from sunshine and from showers,
   Roses, lilies, jessamine;
   And the ivy ran between,
Like a thought in happy hours.

And this feast too lacked no guest,
With its warm delicious rest;
   With its couches softly sinking,
   And its glow not made for thinking,
But for careless joy at best.

Many banqueters were there,
Wrinkled age, the young, the fair;
   In the splendid revelry
   Flushing cheek and kindling eye
Told of gladness without care.

Yet no laughter rang around,
Yet they uttered forth no sound;
  With the smile upon his face
  Each sat moveless in his place,
Silently, as if spellbound.

The low whispering voice was gone,
And I felt awed and alone.
  In my great astonishment
  To the feasters up I went —
Lo they all were turned to stone!

Yea they all were statue-cold,
Men and women, young and old;
  With the life-like look and smile
  And the flush; and all the while
The hard fingers kept their hold.

Here a little child was sitting
With a merry glance, befitting
  Happy age and heedless heart;
  There a young man sat apart,
With a forward look unweeting.

Nigh them was a maiden fair,
And the ringlets of her hair
  Round her slender fingers twined;
  And she blushed as she reclined,
Knowing that her love was there.

Here a dead man sat to sup,
In his hand a drinking cup;
   Wine-cup of the heavy gold,
   Human hand stony and cold,
And no life-breath struggling up.

There a mother lay and smiled
Down upon her infant child;
   Happy child and happy mother,
   Laughing back to one another
With a gladness undefiled.

Here an old man slept, worn out
With the revelry and rout;
   Here a strong man sat and gazed
   On a girl whose eyes upraised
No more wandered roundabout.

And none broke the stillness — none;
I was the sole living one.
   And methought that silently
   Many seemed to look on me
With strange steadfast eyes that shone.

Full of fear I would have fled;
Full of fear I bent my head,
   Shutting out each stony guest. —
   When I looked again, the feast
And the tent had vanished.

Yes, once more I stood alone
Where the happy sunlight shone,
  And a gentle wind was sighing,
  And the little birds were flying,
And the dreariness was gone.

All these things that I have said
Awed me and made me afraid.
  What was I that I should see
  So much hidden mystery?
And I straightway knelt and prayed.

6 *April* 1847.

THE ROSE

O ROSE, thou flower of flowers, thou fragrant wonder,
Who shall describe thee in thy ruddy prime,
 Thy perfect fullness in the summertime,
When the pale leaves blushingly part asunder
And show the warm red heart lies glowing under?
  Thou shouldst bloom surely in some sunny clime,
  Untouched by blights and chilly winter's rime,
Where lightnings never flash nor peals the thunder.
And yet in happier spheres they cannot need thee
  So much as we do with our weight of woe;

Perhaps they would not tend, perhaps not heed thee,
And thou wouldst lonely and neglected grow:
And He who is all wise, He hath decreed thee
To gladden earth and cheer all hearts below.

17 *April* 1847.

I HAVE FOUGHT A GOOD FIGHT

"Who art thou that comest with a steadfast face
Through the hushed arena to the burying-place?"
"I am one whose footprints marked upon the sand
Cry in blood for vengeance on a guilty land."

"How are these thy garments white as whitest snow
Though thy blood hath touched them in its overflow?"
"My blood cannot stain them, nor my tears make white;
One than I more mighty, He hath made them bright."

"Say, do thy wounds pain thee open every one,
Wounds that now are glowing clearer than the sun?"
"Nay, they are my gladness unalloyed by grief;
Like a desert-fountain, or a long relief."

"When the lion had thee in his deadly clasp,
Was there then no terror in thy stifled gasp?"
"Though I felt the crushing, and the grinding teeth,
He was with me ever, He who comforteth."

"Didst thou hear the shouting, as of a great flood,
Crying out for vengeance, crying out for blood?"
"I heard it in silence, and was not afraid,
While for the mad people silently I prayed."

"Did their hate not move thee? art thou heedless then
Of the fear of children and the curse of men?"
"God looked down upon me from the heaven above,
And I did not tremble, happy in His love."

July 1847.

WISHES

OH would that I were very far away
    Among the lanes, with hedges all around,
    Happily listening to the dreamy sound
Of distant sheep-bells, smelling the new hay
And all the wild flowers scattered in my way:
    Or would that I were lying on some mound
    Where shade and butterflies and thyme abound,
Beneath the trees, upon a sunny day:
Or would I strolled beside the mighty sea —
    The sea before, and the tall cliffs behind;
While winds from the warm south might tell to me
    How health and joy for all men are designed: —
But, be I where I may, would I had thee,
    And heard thy gentle voice, my Mother kind.

22 *July* 1847.

THE DREAM

REST, rest; the troubled breast
    Panteth evermore for rest: —
Be it sleep or be it death,
    Rest is all it coveteth.

Tell me, dost thou remember the old time
    We sat together by that sunny stream,
And dreamed our happiness was too sublime
    Only to be a dream?

Gazing, till steadfast gazing made us blind,
    We watched the fishes leaping at their play;
Thinking our love too tender and too kind
    Ever to pass away.

And some of all our thoughts were true at least
    What time we thought together by that stream;
Thy happiness has evermore increased, —
    My love was not a dream.

And, now that thou art gone, I often sit
    On its green margin, for thou once wert there;
And see the clouds that, floating over it,
    Darken the quiet air.

THE DREAM

Yes oftentimes I sit beside it now,
    Harkening the wavelets ripple o'er the sands;
Until again I hear thy whispered vow
    And feel thy pressing hands.

Then the bright sun seems to stand still in heaven,
    The stream sings gladly as it onward flows,
The rushes grow more green, the grass more even,
    Blossoms the budding rose.

I say: "It is a joy-dream; I will take it;
    He is not gone — he will return to me."
What found'st thou in my heart that thou shouldst
    break it? —
    How have I injured thee?

Oh I am weary of life's passing show,
    Its pageant and its pain.
I would I could lie down lone in my woe,
    Ne'er to rise up again;
I would I could lie down where none might know;
    For truly love is vain.
Truly love's vain; but oh how vainer still
    Is that which is not love, but seems!
Concealed indifference, a covered ill,
    A very dream of dreams.

1847.

ELEANOR

CHERRY-RED her mouth was,
    Morning-blue her eye,
Lady-slim her little waist
    Rounded prettily;
And her sweet smile of gladness
    Made every heart rejoice:
But sweeter even than her smile
    The tones were of her voice.

Sometimes she spoke, sometimes she sang;
    And evermore the sound
Floated, a dreamy melody,
    Upon the air around;
As though a wind were singing
    Far up beside the sun,
Till sound and warmth and glory
    Were blended all in one.

Her hair was long and golden,
    And clustered unconfined
Over a forehead high and white
    That spoke a noble mind.
Her little hand, her little foot
    Were ready evermore
To hurry forth to meet a friend;
    She smiling at the door.

But, if she sang or if she spoke,
    'Twas music soft and grand,
As though a distant singing sea
    Broke on a tuneful strand;
As though a blessed Angel
    Were singing a glad song,
Halfway between the earth and heaven
    Joyfully borne along.

30 *July* 1847.

ISIDORA

LOVE, whom I have loved too well,
    Turn thy face away from me;
For I heed nor heaven nor hell
    While mine eyes can look on thee.
Do not answer, do not speak,
For thy voice can make me weak.

I must choose 'twixt God and man,
    And I dare not hesitate:
Oh how little is life's span,
    And Eternity how great!
Go out from me; for I fear
Mine own strength while thou art here.

Husband, leave me; but know this:
   I would gladly give my soul
So that thine might dwell in bliss
   Free from the accurst control,
So that thou mightest go hence
In a hopeful penitence.

Yea from hell I would look up,
   And behold thee in thy place,
Drinking of the living cup,
   With the joy-look on thy face,
And the light that shines alone
From the glory of the Throne.

But how could my endless loss
   Be thine everlasting gain?
Shall thy palm grow from my cross?
   Shall thine ease be in my pain?
Yea thine own soul witnesseth
Thy life is not in my death.

It were vain that I should die —
   That we thus should perish both;
Thou wouldst gain no peace thereby;
   And in truth I should be loth
By the loss of my salvation
To increase thy condemnation.

Little infant, his and mine,
   Would that I were as thou art;

Nothing breaks that sleep of thine,
   And ah nothing breaks thy heart;
And thou knowest naught of strife,
The heart's death for the soul's life.

None misdoubt thee, none misdeem
   Of thy wishes and thy will.
All thy thoughts are what they seem,
   Very pure and very still;
And thou fearest not the voice
That once made thy heart rejoice.

Oh how calm thou art, my child!
   I could almost envy thee.
Thou hast neither wept nor smiled,
   Thou that sleepest quietly.
Would I also were at rest
With the one that I love best.

Husband, go. I dare not harken
   To thy words or look upon
Those despairing eyes that darken
   Down on me — But he is gone!
Nay, come back, and be my fate
As thou wilt! — It is too late.

I have conquered; it is done,
   Yea the death-struggle is o'er,
And the hopeless quiet won: —
   I shall see his face no more: —

And mine eyes are waxing dim
Now they cannot look on him.

And my heart-pulses are growing
  Very weak, and through my whole
Life-blood a slow chill is going: —
  Blessed Saviour, take my soul
To Thy Paradise and care: —
Paradise, will he be there?

9 *August* 1847.

ZARA

NOW the pain beginneth and the word is spoken;—
  Hark unto the tolling of the churchyard
    chime!—
Once my heart was gladsome, now my heart is
    broken, —
  Once my love was noble, now it is a crime.

But the fear is over; yea what now shall pain me?
  Arm thee in thy sorrow, O most desolate!
Weariness and weakness, these shall now sustain me,—
  Pride and bitter grieving, burning love and hate.

Yea the fear is over, the strong fear and trembling;
　I can doubt no longer, he is gone indeed.
Rend thy hair, lost woman, weep without dissembling;
　The heart torn forth from it, shall the breast not bleed?

Happy she who looketh on his beauty's glory!
　Happy she who listeneth to his gentle word!
Yet, O happy maiden, sorrow lies before thee;
　Greeting hath been given, parting must be heard.

He shall leave thee also, he who now hath left me,
　With a weary spirit and an aching heart;
Thou shalt be bereaved by him who hath bereft me;
　Thou hast sucked the honey, — feel the stinging's smart.

Let the cold gaze on him, let the heartless hear him,
　For he shall not hurt them, they are safe in sooth:
But let loving women shun that man and fear him,
　Full of cruel kindness and devoid of ruth.

When ye call upon him, hope for no replying;
　When ye gaze upon him, think not he will look;
Hope not for his pity when your heart is sighing;
　Such another, waiting, weeping, he forsook.

Hath the heaven no thunder wherewith to denounce him?
　Hath the heaven no lightning wherewith to chastise?

O my heart and spirit, O my soul, renounce him
  Who hath called for vengeance from the distant
    skies:

Vengeance which pursues thee, vengeance which shall
    find thee,
  Crushing thy false spirit, scathing thy fair limb:—
O ye thunders, deafen, O ye lightnings, blind me,
  Winds and storms from heaven, strike me but
    spare him!

I forgive thee, dearest, cruel, I forgive thee;—
  May thy cup of sorrow be poured out for me;
Though the dregs be bitter yet they shall not grieve
    me,
  Knowing that I drink them, O my love, for thee.

1847.

THE NOVICE

I LOVE one and he loveth me:
  Who sayeth this? who deemeth this?
And is this thought a cause of bliss,
  Or source of misery?

The loved may die, or he may change:
And if he die thou art bereft;
Or if he alter nought is left
  Save life that seemeth strange.

THE NOVICE

A weary life, a hopeless life,
Full of all ill and fear-oppressed;
A weary life that looks for rest
   Alone after death's strife.

And love's joy hath no quiet even;
It evermore is variable.
Its gladness is like war in hell
   More than repose in heaven.

Yea it is as a poison-cup
That holds one quick fire-draught within;
For when the life seems to begin
   The slow death looketh up.

Then bring me to a solitude
Where love may neither come nor go;
Where very peaceful waters flow,
   And roots are found for food;

Where the wild honey-bee booms by,
And trees and bushes freely give
Ripe fruit and nuts: there I would live,
   And there I fain would die.

There autumn leaves may make my grave,
And little birds sing over it;
And there cool twilight winds may flit
   And shadowy branches wave.

4 *September* 1847.

IMMALEE

I GATHER thyme upon the sunny hills,
And its pure fragrance ever gladdens me,
And in my mind having tranquillity
I smile to see how my green basket fills.
And by clear streams I gather daffodils;
   And in dim woods find out the cherry-tree,
   And take its fruit and the wild strawberry
And nuts and honey; and live free from ills.
I dwell on the green earth, 'neath the blue sky,
   Birds are my friends, and leaves my rustling roof;
The deer are not afraid of me, and I
   Hear the wild goat, and hail its hastening hoof;
The squirrels sit perked as I pass them by,
   And even the watchful hare stands not aloof.

21 *September* 1847.

LADY ISABELLA

HEART warm as summer, fresh as spring,
   Gracious as autumn's harvesting,
Pure as the winter's snows; as white
A hand as lilies in sunlight;
Eyes glorious as a midnight star;
Hair shining as the chestnuts are;

A step firm and majestical;
A voice singing and musical;
A soft expression, kind address;
Tears for another's heaviness;
Bright looks ; an action full of grace;
A perfect form, a perfect face;
All these become a woman well,
And these had Lady Isabel.

27 September 1847.

NIGHT AND DEATH

Now the sunlit hours are o'er,
    Rise up from thy shadowy shore,
Happy Night, whom Chaos bore.

Better is the peaceful treasure
Of thy musings without measure
Than the day's unquiet pleasure.

Bring the holy moon; so pale
She herself seems but a veil
For the sun, where no clouds sail.

Bring the stars, thy progeny;
Each a little lamp on high
To light up an azure sky.

Sounds incomprehensible
In the shining planets dwell
Of thy sister Queen to tell.

Of that sister Nature saith
She hath power o'er life and breath;
And her name is written Death.

She is fairer far than thou;
Grief her head can never bow,
Joy is stamped upon her brow.

She is full of gentleness,
And of faith and hope; distress
Finds in her forgetfulness.

In her arms who lieth down
Never more is seen to frown,
Though he wore a thorny crown.

Whoso sigheth in unrest,
If his head lean on her breast
Witnesseth she is the best.

All the riches of the earth,
Weighed by her, are nothing worth:
She is the eternal birth.

In her treasure-house are found
Stored abundantly around
Almsdeeds done without a sound;

Long forbearance; patient will;
Fortitude in midst of ill;
Hope, when even fear grew still;

Kindness given again for hate;
Hearts resigned though desolate;
Meekness, which is truly great;

Bitter tears of penitence;
Changeless love's omnipotence:—
And nought lacketh recompense.

In her house no tainted thing
Winneth any entering;
There the poor have comforting.

There they wait a little time
Till the Angel-uttered chime
Sound the eternal matin-prime.

Then, upraised in joyfulness,
They shall know her, and confess
She is blessed and doth bless.

When earth's fleeting day is flown,
All created things shall own,
Death is Life, and Death alone.

28 *September* 1847.

THE LOTUS-EATERS

Ulysses to Penelope

IN a far distant land they dwell,
  Incomprehensible,
Who love the shadow more than light,
  More than the sun the moon,
  Cool evening more than noon,
Pale silver more than gold that glitters bright.
  A dark cloud overhangs their land
    Like a mighty hand,
  Never moving from above it;
  A cool shade and moist and dim,
  With a twilight purple rim,
    And they love it.
  And sometimes it giveth rain,
    But soon it ceaseth as before,
  And earth drieth up again,—
    Then the dews rise more and more,
    Till it filleth, dropping o'er;
  But no forked lightnings flit,
  And no thunders roll in it.
  Through the land a river flows,
  With a sleepy sound it goes:
    Such a drowsy noise, in sooth,
      Those who will not listen hear not:
      But, if one is wakeful, fear not—

It shall lull him to repose,
   Bringing back the dreams of youth.
Hemlock groweth, poppy bloweth,
In the fields where no man moweth:
And the vine is full of wine
And are full of milk the kine,
And the hares are all secure,
And the birds are wild no more,
And the forest-trees wax old,
And winds stir, or hot or cold,—
And yet no man taketh care,
All things resting everywhere.

7 *October* 1847.

SONNET

From the Psalms

ALL through the livelong night I lay awake,
   Watering my couch with tears of heaviness.
None stood beside me in my sore distress:—
Then cried I to my heart: If thou wilt, break,
But be thou still; no moaning will I make,
   Nor ask man's help, nor kneel that he may bless.
   So I kept silence in my haughtiness,
Till lo the fire was kindled, and I spake —
Saying: Oh that I had wings like to a dove,
   Then would I flee away and be at rest:

I would not pray for friends or hope or love,
  But still the weary throbbing of my breast:
And, gazing on the changeless heavens above,
  Witness that such a quietness is best.

7 November 1847.

SONG

THE stream moaneth as it floweth,
  The wind sigheth as it bloweth,
Leaves are falling, Autumn goeth,
  Winter cometh back again;
And the air is very chilly,
And the country rough and hilly,
  And I shiver in the rain.
Who will help me? who will love me?
Heaven sets forth no light above me:
Ancient memories reprove me,
Long-forgotten feelings move me,
  I am full of heaviness.
Earth is cold, too cold the sea:
Whither shall I turn and flee?
Is there any hope for me?
Any ease for my heart-aching,
Any sleep that hath no waking,
Any night without day-breaking,
  Any rest from weariness?
Hark the wind is answering:

Hark the running stream replieth:
There is a rest for him that dieth:
In the grave whoever lieth
Nevermore hath sorrowing.
Holy slumber, holy quiet,
Close the eyes and still the riot:
And the brain forgets its thought,
   And the heart forgets its beating.
   Earth and earthly things are fleeting;
There is what all men have sought —
Long unchangeable repose,
Lulling us from many woes.

7 November 1847.

THE WORLD'S HARMONIES

OH listen, listen, for the Earth
   Hath silent melody:
Green grasses are her lively chords,
   And blossoms: and each tree,
Chestnut and oak and sycamore,
   Makes solemn harmony.

Oh listen, listen, for the Sea
   Is calling unto us:
Her notes are the broad liquid waves
   Mighty and glorious.
Lo the first man and the last man
   Hath heard, shall hearken thus.

The Sun on which men cannot look,
    Its splendour is so strong,
Which wakeneth life and giveth life,
    Rolling in light along,
From day-dawn to dim eventide
    Sings the eternal song.

And the Moon taketh up the hymn,
    And the Stars answer all:
And all the Clouds and all the Winds
    And all the Dews that fall
And Frost and fertilizing Rain
    Are mutely musical.

Fishes and Beasts and feathered Fowl
    Swell the eternal chaunt,
That riseth through the lower air,
    Over the rainbow slant,
Up through the unseen palace-gates,
    Fearlessly jubilant.

Before the everlasting Throne
    It is acceptable:
It hath no pause or faltering:
    The Angels know it well:
Yea in the highest heaven of heavens
    Its sound is audible.

Yet than the voice of the whole World
  There is a sweeter voice,
That maketh all the Cherubim
  And Seraphim rejoice:
That all the blessed Spirits hail
  With undivided choice:

That crieth at the golden door
  And gaineth entrance in:
That the palm-branch and radiant crown
  And glorious throne may win: —
The lowly prayer of a Poor Man
  Who turneth from his sin.

20 *November* 1847.

THE LAST ANSWER

(Written to Bouts-rimés)

SHE turned round to me with her steadfast eyes.
  "I tell you I have looked upon the dead;
Have kissed the brow and the cold lips," she said;
"Have called upon the sleeper to arise.
He loved me, yet he stirred not: on this wise,
  Not bowing in weak agony my head,
  But all too sure of what life is, to dread,
Learned I that love and hope are fallacies."

> She gazed quite calmly on me: and I felt
> > Awed and astonished and almost afraid:
> > > For what was I to have admonished her?
> > Then, being full of doubt and fear, I knelt,
> > And tears came to my eyes even as I prayed:
> > > But she meanwhile only grew statelier.

2 *December* 1847.

NOTES

BY WILLIAM M. ROSSETTI

REPINING, page 4.—This poem was published in *The Germ*, 1850. It is, of all the poems by Christina Rossetti which appeared in that short-lived magazine, the only one which she did not afterwards reprint. No doubt it is far from being excellent; yet it cannot be called bad, and I think the time has now come for giving it a modest place amid the authoress's writings. In her MS. it is very considerably longer than in *The Germ*, or hence in the present volume: the curtailment was a highly judicious act. The reader will readily perceive that this poem is to some extent modelled upon Parnell's *Hermit*. The moral, however, is different. Parnell aims to show that the dispensations of Providence, though often mysterious, are just. Christina's thesis might be summarized thus: Solitude is dreary, yet the life of man among his fellows may easily be drearier; therefore let not the solitary rebel.

Lady Montrevor, page 14.—This sonnet applies to a personage in Maturin's novel, *The Wild Irish Boy*. Christina, as well as her brothers, was in early youth very fond of Maturin's novels, and more than one of her poems relates to these. Lady Montrevor is possibly now almost forgotten. She is a brilliant woman of the world who fascinates "the Wild Irish Boy," and leads both him and herself into grave dilemmas.

Twelve Sonnets written to Bouts-rimés, page 15.—Our brother Dante Gabriel and myself were, towards 1848, greatly addicted to writing sonnets together to *bouts-rimés;* most of my verses published in *The Germ*—and this remark applies not to sonnets alone — were thus composed. I hardly know whether I ought to be ashamed or the contrary to confess the fact; it extenuates some of the obvious faults of the verses, but it shows that I was rather trifling with my reader. Christina did not do much in the like way; but, being in my company at Brighton in the summer of 1848, she consented to try her chance. Like her brothers, she was very rapid at the work. The first sonnet in this present series was done in nine minutes; the ninth in five. After the Brighton days she renewed this exercise little, if at all. A few of her *bouts-rimés* sonnets, after the first scribbling of them, were retouched to some, but only a small, extent.

Sonnet vii, page 18. — This sonnet about a chilly August is certainly not a marked success; but I suppose it pictured with some truth the day on which it was written, and I allow it to pass muster.

Sonnet viii, page 19. — Dante Rossetti, writing on 30 August 1848, said, in relation to one of Christina's *bouts-rimés* sonnets (I am not certain which): " Her other is first-rate. Pray impress upon her that this and the one beginning ' Methinks the ills of life ' [*i.e.* No. 8] are as good as anything she has written, and well worthy of revision."

The Plague, page 20. — Dante Rossetti's letter above-mentioned says of this sonnet: " I grinned tremendously over Christina's *Plague*, which however is forcible, and has something good in it."

Sonnets x a, b, and c, pages 20, 21, 22. — The sonnet marked *c* was, like 1 to 9, written at Brighton. At a later date — 1850, or perhaps earlier — Christina wrote a prose story for girls, entitled *Maude* (it has not been published). An incident in this story is the competition of three young ladies composing *bouts-rimés* sonnets; *c* is pronounced to be the best of the three. The sonnet *a* (it will at once be observed) is not a true sonnet at all, having lines of unequal length. This was, of course, intentional on Christina's part, to mark the inaptitude of the young lady who is supposed to have indited *a*. None the less I give the three sonnets together, as showing how readily Christina could utilize the same rhymes for three entirely distinct lines of thought or subject. Two of the phrases in *c* are thus commented in *Maude :* " I have literally seen [and this I know to be a fact] a man in Regent Street wearing a sort of hooked cloak with one tassel. Of course every one will understand 'the Bason' to mean the one in St. James's Park."

To Lalla, page 25. — This was a pet name given to Henrietta Polydore, daughter of our Uncle Henry. The name was her own baby invention, I think. She became consumptive, and died in America in 1874, aged about twenty-eight.

Three Nuns, page 27. — The second section of this poem was the first written, standing then as a separate composition. The united poem was inserted into the prose tale *Maude*, with the observation: " Pray read the mottoes; put together, they form a most exquisite little song which the nuns sing in Italy."

The End of the First Part, page 36. — This appears to be a personal utterance. As to what condition of facts it was founded on I feel no assurance, unless we are to regard it simply as an indication of deepening religious convictions, and consequent alienation from mundane interests and desires. "Tears for guilt" is, in reference to Christina, a very exaggerated phrase; or possibly nothing is implied beyond "original guilt" or "original sin."

Two Enigmas, page 37. — The answer to the first of these enigmas is "Jack." It was published in a little pocket-book named *Marshall's Ladies' Daily Remembrancer* for 1850, and must apparently (according to the conditions laid down) have been sent in before June 1849. One copy of the *Remembrancer* was awarded as a prize to the authoress; some other more admired contributors received two copies. The second enigma means "Punch," which was another of the subjects for the *Remembrancer* of 1850. This second enigma has reached me only in a manuscript copy made by one of our aunts.

Two Charades, page 38. — The first means " Proserpine," the second " Candid." The latter was published in the *Remembrancer* aforenamed. There was another unpublished charade, *Ægisthus;* but I have not thought it deserving of type.

Looking Forward, page 40. — The tone of this lyric suggests that it was written in expectation of seemingly imminent death; it stands in my mother's handwriting (quite contrary to wont), and so does another poem — long ago published — dated in the same month. Christina's health — even perhaps as early as the age of eighteen or seventeen — was often exceedingly frail, and no member of the family then looked for her living out an ordinary length of years.

Queen Rose, page 42.—Christina sang often—possibly too often—the praises of the rose; she regarded it not merely in its own beauty, but as the symbol of love, whether construed as deep human affection or as union with the Divine. The lily stood with her (as with so many another) for faith.

Is and Was, page 50.—The last line of this poem, "Doing all from self-respect," may be worth a moment's comment. Much about the time when the poem was written, a lady told my sister that the latter seemed to "do all from self-respect," not from fellow-feeling with others, or from kindly consideration for them. Christina mentioned the remark, with an admission that it hit a blot in her character, in which a certain amount of reserve and distance, not remote from *hauteur*, was certainly at that date perceptible. She laid the hint to heart, and, I think, never forgot it.

Annie, page 52.—Christina, the most scrupulous of women and of writers, put to this lyric a note—"query Borrows." She meant that there may, or possibly may not, be here some unconscious reminiscences from other poems.

Books in the Running Brooks, page 56.—This was printed in some magazine; I know neither the name nor the date of the latter. In MS. it stands entitled *After a Picture in the Portland Gallery*. What this picture may have been I cannot now say; not one by Dante Rossetti, who did not exhibit in that gallery after 1850.

To what Purpose is this Waste? page 61.—Twelve lines out of this composition, not a little altered in diction (beginning "Innocent eyes not ours"), were published, under the title *These all wait upon Thee*, in the volume *Verses* of 1893 (Society for Promoting Christian Knowledge). I include these lines, in the form which they bear in the MS., being authorized by the Society to do so—and two similar instances occur further on.

Next of Kin, page 66.—This appears to be a personal address to some very youthful relative; if so, it can only be intended for the "Lalla" named in a previous note, for Christina had no other relative younger than herself.

Portraits, page 67.—This warm-hearted though light effusion is meant for myself in the first stanza, and for Dante Gabriel and myself in the last. There used to be an intermediate stanza, characterizing *him;* it is torn out (by his rather arbitrary hand, beyond a doubt), and I do not remember its terms. Many readers now will agree with me in thinking this a great pity. A laudatory phrase or two regarding myself ought possibly to have induced me to exclude the verses, but I cannot make up my mind to do that.

What? page 68. — The answer to the query appears to be "Youthful Love." This is the first piece in the present collection which points with some distinctness to an unhappy love-passage in my sister's life. While on the one hand I have no intention of entering into precise details, I see on the other no use in making a mystery of such a matter. A few words of explanation clear up several passages in her writings which might otherwise remain open to conjecture equally vague and vain, and possibly not pleasant. My sister was twice sought in marriage; and in each instance was well disposed to her suitor, but was withheld by religious considerations. The first suitor, a painter, was a Christian, but not in the Anglican communion; the second, a scholar and literary man — and this was far the more serious affair of the two — either was not a Christian at all, or else was a Christian of undefined and heterodox views. The first matter terminated towards 1850, the second towards 1864. Both the men died during Christina's lifetime.

Near the Styx, page 69. — These sportive lines take their cue, of course, from the old song "In my cottage near the wood." They tickled our sister Maria uncommonly. I had totally forgotten them; Christina on her deathbed (9 October 1894) happened to recite them to me — for she was often extremely conversible up to and beyond that date, spite of her pain and languor — and I wrote them down from her lips.

For Rosaline's Album, page 74. — Rosaline was Miss Orme, who, not long after the date of these verses, married Professor David Masson, now Queen's Historiographer for Scotland. I am not sure as to the actual date of the verses; it was not later than September 1853, when they, and a few others hereabouts, were copied out by my sister under the general heading *Odds and Ends*. These sepulchral verses are perhaps not quite the staple for a very youthful (and I might add charming) lady's album.

Restive, page 79. — In July 1854 my sister put together, under the general title *Three Stages*, a trio of separate compositions. The first is the one which has been published under the title *A Pause of Thought* ("I looked for that which is not, nor can be"); it was written on 14 February 1848, and was then named *Lines in Memory of Schiller's Der Pilgrim*. The second appears in the present volume as *The End of the First Part*, its date being 18 April 1849. The third is our present item, to which I have supplied the title *Restive*. Considering that No. 1 has already been published, I do not reprint it here; and this induces me to leave No. 2 under its proper date, and to print No. 3 as an independent lyric. Perhaps at some future time it might be best to relink the three together, recurring to the title *Three Stages*.

To the End, page 91. — The last quatrain of this poem seems to present a certain reminiscence (yet far from being a plagiarism) from Dante Rossetti's early achievement *The Blessed Damozel*.

Look on this Picture and on This, page 103. — In my sister's MS. this poem is a rather long one, forty-six triplets; I have reduced it to twenty-three — omitting those passages which appear to me to be either in themselves inferior, or adapted rather for spinning out the theme than intensifying it. Longer or shorter, the poem is perhaps hardly up to the writer's mark; but there is a degree of peculiarity about it which disinclines me to drop it out. Were it not for the name "Eva," I should be embarrassed to guess what could have directed my sister's pen to so singular a subject and treatment; but that name satisfies me that she was here recurring to a favourite romancist of her girlhood, Maturin (see note to p. 14). In Maturin's novel entitled *Women* there is a personage Eva, and a situation which must certainly have prompted the present poem.

Gone Before, page 108. — This was printed in some magazine; I cannot now say which nor when.

Winter, page 112. — Mr. Swynfen Jervis, a friendly acquaintance of our father, wrote a quatrain and a half entitled *Sir Winter;* and he appears to have got Christina to complete the little poem. Christina finished quatrain two, and wrote five others. The third of these five reverts to the idea of "*Sir Winter*"; so I omit it, as being extraneous to the character of her own composition: it has no poetical value.

A Triad, page 113. — This very fine sonnet was published in the volume of 1862, *Goblin Market and other Poems*, but was omitted in subsequent issues. I presume that my sister, with overstrained scrupulosity, considered its moral tone to be somewhat open to exception. In such a view I by no means agree, and I therefore reproduce it.

In an Artist's Studio, page 114.—The reference is apparently to our brother's studio, and to his constantly-repeated heads of the lady whom he afterwards married, Miss Siddal.

A Nightmare (Fragment), page 118.—In my sister's note-book this composition begins on p. 25, and ends on p. 27; the intermediate leaf has been torn out. Mere scrap as it is, I should be sorry to lose it quite.

For One Sake, page 119.—If this is to be regarded as a personal utterance, I know not to what it can point. The phrase "Wars and rumours of your wars" suggests to me that it may *possibly* have something to do with the Indian Mutiny of 1857.

From Metastasio, page 120. — These lines form a paraphrastic translation from a lyric ("Amo te solo") in Metastasio's *Clemenza di Tito*. I found them as a scrap of MS., pencilled by Christina thus: "I must have done this for Traventi, who wanted English words to set to music." Traventi was a Neapolitan musical composer and teacher, whom we knew after my father's death in 1854; the date of the translation may be 1857 — or earlier rather than later.

Yet a Little While, page 122.—In the MS. note-book the last two stanzas of this lyric are cancelled by a pencil-line. In this line I seem to trace the "Roman hand" of my brother, not my sister. Those stanzas comprise some verses which I should be loth to lose, so I retain them. Two other stanzas, the third and fourth, were used by Christina in the *Verses*, 1893, with the title *Vanity of Vanities*. They are there modified in diction and lyrical form, and I reproduce what I find in the MS. note-book.

Father and Lover, page 124.—These two songs — the first spoken by the Father, and the second by the Lover — come from a prose fairy-tale named *Hero*, which was printed in the volume entitled *Commonplace and Other Stories*, 1870 — long out of print. I am not sure as to when my sister wrote *Hero;* but I take it to have been several years prior to 1870.

Cousin Kate, page 127.—This composition shared the fate of *A Triad* (see note to p. 113), and I presume for a like reason.

Sister Maude, page 129.—Similar to the preceding. I am not certain as to the date of this forcible poem.

Better So, page 131.—It seems probable that this lyric was written upon the death of some cherished friend; I do not remember who it was. The date is not consistent with any death in our own family. The next poem relates of course to the decease of the Prince Consort. It might be possible to suppose that Christina wrote the present lines as an appropriate utterance for "Our Widowed Queen." The Prince indeed died on 14 (not 13) December, but on the 13th his death was clearly anticipated.

In Progress, page 134.—The expressions in this sonnet, if used by some one else, might have been not far from apposite to Christina herself. I do not, however, consider that she wrote the verses with any such reference. Clearly the sonnet describes some particular person; I can think of two ladies not wholly unlike this touching portrait—one more especially whom Christina first knew in Newcastle-on-Tyne. But any such guess may be quite wrong.

Seasons, page 135.—These lines were published in *Macmillan's Magazine*. They show a shrinking from winter-time, apparent in several other compositions. Italian blood may partly account for this; yet, after all, there is plenty of beauty in an ordinary winter, English or other, and the sensations of an invalid (troubled up to early middle age with many symptoms which seemed to point towards consumption) may have had more to do with the feeling.

Helen Grey, page 138.—Published in *Macmillan's Magazine*.

Last Night, page 144.—Similar.

If, page 145.—This also was published in some magazine—I think it was named *The Shilling Magazine*. Mr. Frederick A. Sandys made a very able design to it, engraved on wood; able, but (to my thinking) not in character with the poem.

En Route, page 152.—Under this heading I find three pieces which seem to have little connection one with the other. Presumably they were all written while my sister, along with my mother and myself, was making a flying visit to North Italy (through France and Switzerland). She was never there at any other time. The passionate delight in Italy to which the second section of *En Route* bears witness suggests that she was almost an alien — or, like her father, an exile — in the North. She never perhaps wrote anything better. I can remember the intense relief and pleasure with which she saw loveable Italian faces and heard musical Italian speech at Bellinzona after the somewhat hard and nipped quality of the German Swiss.

Husband and Wife, page 154. — This was published in a book called *A Masque of Poets;* I do not recollect the details. It appears to be the same poem which (as shown in a letter from my brother, 5 January 1866, published in his *Family-letters*) Mr. F. A. Sandys was thinking of illustrating, and for which my brother proposed the title *Grave-clothes and Baby-clothes*.

Love's Name, page 161. — This small ditty — unimportant, and yet melodious — is introduced into the prose tale named *Commonplace*, finished in 1870, and published in the same year. It is supposed to be sung by certain young ladies in Greek costume, enacting a charade upon the word "Love-apple."

An Echo from Willow-wood, page 164. — The title indicates that this sonnet by Christina is based on those sonnets by our brother, named *Willow-wood*, which were first published in 1869. I incline to think that Christina's sonnet is intended to refer to the love and marriage of my brother and Miss Siddal, and to her early death in 1862. The verses were printed in some magazine (perhaps *The Magazine of Art*), with an illustration by Mr. C. Ricketts.

Golden Holly, page 165. — This trifle, owing to its associations of old and uninterrupted friendship, I am unwilling to omit. It was addressed to Holman [Holly] Frederic Stephens, then a little boy, son of our constant friend, Frederic George Stephens (one of the seven members of the "P.R.B."). Tennyson once saw the child in the Isle of Wight, and pronounced him (not unreasonably) to be "the most beautiful boy I have ever seen." Mr. Stephens senior, in sending me the verses at my request, wrote that they refer "to H. F. S.'s frequent pet name of 'the Golden Holly,' given because of the brightness of his long hair, as well as his birthday being on October 31. He had sent a tea-rose to C. G. R."

An Alphabet, page 165. — This was printed in 1875, with some woodcuts, in some magazine; the headline of the pages is *For Very Little Folks*, which may or may not be the title of the magazine itself. It must be an American publication, as the verses are headed *An Alphabet from England*.

Cor Mio, page 168. — I find this sonnet in my sister's handwriting, endorsed by her "the original version of my sonnet." The reference is to a sonnet in her volume of 1881, *A Pageant and Other Poems* — being No. 18 in the series named *Later Life*. In that printed version the octave (beginning "So late in autumn half the world's asleep") is entirely changed, while the sestett remains the same. The present form of this sonnet, being a more directly personal utterance, seems worth preserving.

Who Shall Say? page 168. — These lines (I supply a title to them) were written in the rough on a scrap of paper. There is nothing to suggest that they are incomplete, and they are certainly not bad, so I insert them. Date merely conjectural.

Life, page 169. — This sonnet was written on the back of the preceding lines. The page is partly torn off, so that the first line of the sonnet begins with the half-word "lerable," the second with "ted"; two of the lines, however, are complete. I do not think I can have made any grave mistake in the words which I supply, and there is an energy of tone in the sonnet which indisposes me to reject it.

Lines, page 171. — Like the preceding, these verses are partly curtailed in the slip of MS., some rhyme-words being docked. I have no doubt as to what they ought to be, unless in regard to "thing" (line 7), which is made to rhyme with "everything." But no word except "thing" appears to be even plausible.

Hadrian's Death-Song Translated, page 171. — In 1876 Mr. David Johnston, of Bath, formed the project of collecting various translations of the famous lines — "Animula vagula blandula," etc., and publishing them in a volume, which was privately printed. He looked up old translations, and invited new ones. Christina became one of his contributors, also our sister Maria and myself; Christina making an Italian as well as an English translation, see page 288.

Valentines to my Mother, page 172. — I shall probably not be alone in considering these as very charming compositions of their simple intimate kind. Christina left a pencilled note about them thus: "These Valentines had their origin from my dearest mother's remarking that she had never received one. I, her C. G. R., ever after supplied one on the day; and (so far as I recollect) it was a surprise every time, she having forgotten all about it in the interim." Our mother was born in April 1800, so she was nearly seventy-six when the first Valentine was written: she died in April 1886.

Valentine for 1877, page 172. — The signature "C. G. for M. F. R." means that these verses are spoken as in the person of Maria Francesca (our elder sister) in heaven; she had died in November 1876.

Valentine for 1878, page 173. — This is marked on the back "To the Queen of Hearts," and the like with all the ensuing Valentines.

Valentine for 1883, page 176. — Here is an evident reminiscence as to the death of Dante Gabriel in April 1882; probably also as to the death of my infant son Michael in January 1883.

My Mouse, page 178. — This was not a "mouse" in the ordinary sense, but a "*sea*-mouse." A friend very dear to my sister had picked it up on the seashore, and presented it to her preserved in spirits. The sea-mouse was with her to the end, and will probably remain with me to the end; its brilliant iridescent hues are still vivid.

A Poor Old Dog, page 179. — My sister was a very staunch supporter of the Anti-Vivisection Movement. In a letter to our brother (dated perhaps in 1879) she sent the present verses, with the following remarks: — "There has just been held a fancy sale at a house in Prince's Gate for the Anti-Vivisection cause, and, having nothing else to contribute, I sent a dozen autographs as follows [then come the verses]. Of these, nine on the first day fetched 2s. 6d. or 3s., while one even brought in 10s.! The remaining three, I hope, were disposed of on the closing day."

Parted, page 179. — In 1880 a volume of poems was privately printed. One of its items was entitled *Moor and Christian*, purporting to be "taken from a Spanish source," and expressing the emotion of a Moslem woman severed from her Christian lover. Christina, using the same metre and number of lines, wrote the present composition — of course from a very diverse point of view.

To-day's Burden, page 180. — Comes from Mr. Hall Caine's compilation, *Sonnets of Three Centuries*, 1882. Date conjectural, but probably not far wrong.

Counterblast on Penny Trumpet, page 181. — These rather neat verses are entirely out of my sister's ordinary line, which fact (trifling as they are) makes me the more unwilling to leave them out. They stand signed "C. G. R.: see *St. James's Gazette*, 21 July 1882: motive, a Poem." I infer (for I have not been at the pains of looking up the *St. James's Gazette*) that that newspaper contained some effusion censuring Mr. Bright for having quitted the Ministry after the bombardment of Alexandria, and also censuring Mr. Gladstone for continuing in the Ministry. My sister knew and cared next to nothing about party politics (apart from questions having a religious bearing); in all her later years, however, her feeling leaned more towards the Conservative than the Liberal cause.

Michael F. M. Rossetti, page 181. — These verses were published in the *Athenæum* soon after the death of my infant Michael. They were printed as one consecutive composition, but are properly four separate snatches.

The Way of the World, page 183. — Comes from *The Magazine of Art*, July 1894, and must be the latest printed of any verse composition within my sister's lifetime. Mr. Britten made an illustration to the stanzas. When they were written is quite uncertain to me — possibly at a date even later than that which I have noted.

To my Fior-di-lisa, page 183. — One of the friends who saw my sister most frequently and affectionately in her closing years was Miss Lisa Wilson. Christina sometimes called her Fior-di-lisa (which is the same as Fleur-de-lys). Miss Wilson, who has a graceful touch of her own both in verse and in painting, presented to Christina in 1892 a little illuminated book of poems by herself; my sister inserted into it the present lines of response.

Sleeping at Last, page 184. — I regard these verses (the title is mine) as being the very last that Christina ever wrote; probably late in 1893 or it may be early in 1894. They form a very fitting close to her poetic performance, the longing for rest (even as distinguished from actual bliss in heaven) being most marked throughout the whole course of her writings. I found the lines after her death, and had the gratification of presenting them, along with the childish script of her very first verses *To my Mother*, to the MS. Department of the British Museum.

Behold, I stand at the Door and Knock, page 198. — These verses were published in some magazine. I fancy it may have been one named *Aikin's Year*, with which Mary Howitt was connected. If so, I think the poem must be of a date not later than 1852, the publication not later than 1854; and these would be the first verses by Christina which got into print after the cessation of *The Germ* in 1850.

St. Elizabeth of Hungary, page 204. — I take it that this lyric received its immediate inspiration from the picture of like subject painted by James Collinson.

A Harvest, page 212. — In the MS. note-book the title is *Annie*, and the poem extends to twenty stanzas. It then took the form of an address to "Annie" by a husband or lover; possibly the poignantly-pathetic lines of Edgar Poe, *For Annie*, were partly in my sister's mind. At some later date she numbered five out of the twenty stanzas, evidently contemplating to retain those five alone. I follow her lead, and supply a new title. The poem as it originally stood is, however, by no means a bad one.

The Eleventh Hour, page 214. — This was printed in some magazine; I am unable to give the details.

There remaineth therefore a Rest, page 217. — In the note-book this composition numbers twelve stanzas; two of them, under the title *The Bourne*, were eventually published ("Underneath the growing grass," etc.). The remaining ten were not unworthy to pair with those two, but I think it best to use only five of them.

Ye have forgotten the Exhortation, page 218. — Our father having died on 26 April 1854, it is not unnatural to think that this poem, dated 10 May 1854, bears some direct relation to that loss. There had been two other deaths in the family, May and December 1853, those of our maternal grandparents; to her grandfather especially Christina was most warmly attached.

Hymn after Gabriele Rossetti, page 223. — In our father's volume of religious poems *L'Arpa Evangelica* (1852) there is a composition named *Nell' Atto della Comunione*, in three parts. The third begins with the words — " T' amo, e fra dolci affanni," and is the one which Christina here translates in two separate versions. The date which I give is conjectural; I assume the translation to have been made not long after our father's death. The copy of the *Arpa Evangelica* into which these versions were inserted is profusely illustrated with pencil-designs by Christina.

A Christmas Carol for my Godchildren, page 230. — Christina, from time to time, acted as godmother to various children — mostly, I think, children of poor people in the neighbourhood of Christ Church, Albany Street, Regent's Park. It may be worth noting that this Carol was written not at Christmas time, but early in October; and in many instances a reference to dates would show that poems about festivals of the Church, or about seasons of the year, were written at dates by no means corresponding.

The Heart Knoweth its own Bitterness, page 233. — Few things written by Christina contain more of her innermost self than this. In her volume *Verses* (published by the Society for Promoting Christian Knowledge) she took the first and last stanzas of this vehement utterance, and, altering the metre observably, and the diction not a little, she published them, with the title, *Whatsoever is right, that shall ye receive*.

Only Believe, page 239. — There were originally some other lines concluding this poem. They appear in the *Verses*, 1893, under the title, *What good shall my Life do me?*

A Shadow of Dorothea, page 240. — I do not find in the legend of St. Dorothea any incident corresponding closely to this. I understand that, in the poem, the speaker is a human soul, not as yet confirmed in saintliness, appealing to the flower-bearing Angel of the legend, or rather indeed to the Saviour Christ.

For Henrietta Polydore, page 242. — Christina's title only says " H. P.," but the lines are certainly intended for Henrietta Polydore, our cousin (see note to p. 25). She was born in England and brought up a Roman Catholic. By a curious train of circumstances, she was at one time, while still a child, in Salt

Lake City with the Mormons. Her father recovered her thence, at a time when a military expedition was sent by the Federal Government to control affairs in the Territory of Utah; and the present lines were presumably written by Christina when she heard that her youthful cousin was about to re-embark for England.

Ash Wednesday, page 242. — These verses — bearing no title beyond *Jesus, do I love Thee?* — were printed in the *Lyra Eucharistica*, 1864. *Ash Wednesday* is the authoress's own title in her MS. note-book; I retain it, as the lines were evidently written towards the date of that fast. Preceding the last quatrain, the MS. gives six verses of ecstatic religious appeal which, as they were not printed, I with some hesitation omit.

A Christmas Carol, page 244. — This was in the *Lyra Messianica*, 1865, named simply *Before the paling of the stars*. I retain my sister's own title.

Easter Even, page 245. — Also from the *Lyra Messianica*.

The Offering of the New Law, page 247. — From the *Lyra Eucharistica*.

Within the Veil, page 250. — From the *Lyra Messianica*. These verses would seem to refer to the recent death of some religious and cherished young friend; I cannot now say who it was. In MS. the title of the verses is *One Day*.

Conference between Christ, the Saints, and the Soul, page 253. — Was printed in *Lyra Eucharistica*. I do not find this poem in MS., and infer that it may have been produced while the book was in actual course of preparation. On this ground I date it "*circa* 1863."

Come unto Me, page 255. — From *Lyra Eucharistica*.

Birds of Paradise, page 257. — This was printed in *Lyra Messianica*, under the title *Paradise in a Symbol*. In that volume the substituted title is appropriate, because another poem by Christina is there, named *Paradise in a Dream* ("Once in a dream I saw the flowers," etc.), which has been reprinted ere now. For the present poem her own title in MS. was *Birds of Paradise*, which I prefer to retain here. In the MS. the last line of stanza one stands "Windy-winged they came."

I reproduce the printed phrase, yet am sorry to lose the written one.

I know you not, page 258. — From *Lyra Messianica;* date conjectural.

Thou art the same, and Thy words shall not fail, page 260. — This comes from *The Children's Hymn-book*, edited by Bishop How and others, and published by Messrs. Rivington. The date of publication is not given; I infer it to be 1881, and I therefore date this poem "*circa* 1880." The words are set to be sung to the tune "Grasmere" by Mr. Cameron W. H. Brock.

A Christmas Carol, page 261. — Here again the date is conjectural. The lines appeared in *The Century-Guild Hobby-horse* for 1887.

Cardinal Newman, page 261. — Published in the *Athenæum* for 16 August 1890.

Yea I have a goodly Heritage, page 262. — Published in *Atalanta* for October 1890. Date conjectural.

A Death of a First-born, page 263. — It will readily be perceived that this relates to the death of the Duke of Clarence. The lines were printed in *Literary Opinion*, February 1892.

Faint yet Pursuing, page 264. — These sonnets also were published in *Literary Opinion*, April 1892. Date conjectural.

Heaven Overarches, page 265. — I found these verses rather roughly written in a little memorandum-book. Their date must, I think, be as late as 1893. Except *Sleeping at Last* (p. 184), they appear to be about the last lines produced by my sister.

Versi, page 269. — In 1851–52 some young ladies (mostly living in the Regent's Park neighbourhood) had a fancy for getting up a little privately-printed magazine, which was termed *The Bouquet from Marylebone Gardens*. My sister was invited to contribute, and she consented to do so, writing always in Italian. Each contributor adopted some floral name as a signature; Christina was "Calta." These *Versi*, and also the following two compositions, come from this rather obscure source. Christina's principal contribution was in prose, not verse — a *Corrispondenza Famigliare* between two supposed young ladies,

Italian and English, the former being at school. There are eight of these letters, rather neat performances in their way; and, no doubt, others would have followed but for the early decease of the magazine, the withering of the *Bouquet*.

Nigella, page 270. — In the *Corrispondenza* above-named these verses are introduced as being written by the Italian damsel to accommodate her English friend, who had been asked to produce some Italian lines for a lady's album.

Chiesa e Signore, page 271. — These lines appear in a scrap of MS. which is thus inscribed: — " Written out at Folkestone 6 August 1871, but date of composition not recollected by C. G. R." I infer that the date of composition was then rather remote, perhaps towards 1860.

Il Rosseggiar dell' Oriente, page 272. — For any quasi-explanation as to these singularly pathetic verses — " Love's very vesture and elect disguise," the inborn idiom of a pure and impassioned heart — I refer the reader to my slight remarks upon the poem entitled *What?* page 68. The Italian verses were kept by Christina in the jealous seclusion of her writing-desk, and I suppose no human eye had looked upon them until I found them there after her death.

Blumine risponde, page 274. — In "Blumine" the reader will recognize a name used by Carlyle in *Sartor Resartus*.

Lassuso il caro Fiore, page 276. — The main topic in this little poem must have some relation to what is touched upon in No. 3 of the series.

Per Preferenza, page 282. — To the first of these stanzas Christina has written the word "Supposto"; to the second, "Accertato"; to the third, "Dedotto." There must have been in her head some whimsical notion of logical sequence, or what not. I can understand it to some extent, without discussing it.

L' Uommibatto, page 287. — Christina took it upon her to Italianize in this form the name of the *Wombat*, which was a cherished pet animal of our brother. It will be understood that she is exhorting the Wombat not to follow (which he was much inclined to do) his inborn propensity for burrowing, and not to turn up in the Antipodes, his native Australia.

Adriano, page 288. — See the note to page 171.

Ninna-nanna, page 288. — The following snatches of Italian verse are translations or paraphrases made by Christina from her own volume of nursery songs (several of which, indeed, are fit for apartments other than the nursery) named *Singsong*. Our cousin Teodorico Pietrocola-Rossetti first made some translations from that book, whose title he rendered as *Ninna-nanna;* herein I follow his lead. His translations were felicitous. Inspirited by his example, Christina made other — and I conceive, in poetic essentials, still better — translations. Readers familiar with *Singsong* will perceive that numerous compositions in that volume remain untranslated.

Sognando, page 302. — I give this title to two stanzas which I find written by Christina into a copy of our father's book of sacred poems — *Il Tempo, ovvero Dio e l' Uomo, Salterio*, 1843. The copy is one which he gave in the same year to his sister-in-law, Charlotte Polidori; as the latter lived on till January 1890, this copy would only at that date have become Christina's property. This consideration and also the look of the hand-writing induce me to suppose that the verses were written not earlier than 1890; they would thus be the last Italian verses which my sister ever wrote. She has signed them thus: "C. G. R., fired by papa's calling this metre difficult" — the metre being the one adopted throughout the whole book *Il Tempo* in its original form. This MS. note might suggest a far earlier date for the lines; but, on the whole, I abide by my own view as just expressed.

To my Mother, on the Anniversary of her Birth, page 305. — These are (I believe, beyond a doubt) the first verses that Christina ever composed; written as they were on 27 April 1842, she was then aged eleven years and a third. She was a wayward child; not at all a bookish one, although she read some few things with zest. I presume that we were all a little surprised at her "coming out" in this line, but have no express recollection of details. Our grandfather, Gaetano Polidori, who kept a private printing-press, printed the lines at once on a card; he afterwards, 1847, included them in the small volume named *Verses*. I need not say that the lines are regarded by me as in no sense approaching towards excellence; they are simple, spontaneous, and in some degree neat, and the circumstances seem to warrant their being given here. In the first of Christina's note-books (see remarks in my preface) these two quatrains appear, and the dates for later productions go on to 3 December 1845; and my mother has written on the flyleaf the following "N.B.," which may be worth quoting:—"These verses are truly and literally by my little daughter, who scrupulously rejected all assistance in her rhyming efforts, under the impression that in that case they would not be really her own." At some date—it may have been towards 1850—Christina took it into her head to make some little coloured illustrations to that printed volume of *Verses;* they are slight and amateurish—one might indeed say childish. There is a certain degree of fancy in them, however; and Dante Gabriel always considered that our sister, had she chosen to study and take pains, might have done something as an artist. To the present small poem the emblem is two sprigs of heartsease. As I proceed I shall mention other devices, whenever they seem to present any point of interest.

Hymn, page 305.—This seems to be the fourth thing which Christina wrote in verse. In the note-book there is only one intermediate composition—its inscribed date 1842. There was also (but these were not deemed worthy of a place in the note-book) the jocular couplets on *The Chinaman*, which appear in my Memoir of Dante G. Rossetti. So far as I can make out, that *Chinaman* was the first thing which Christina wrote after the verses *To my Mother*.

Love Ephemeral, page 309.—Device—the crescent moon, with a lunar (more like a solar) rainbow.

Burial Anthem, page 310.—This may, or may not, have been written in relation to some one in particular; there was not any death in our immediate family about that date. Device —a sprig of blue and pink forget-me-not.

The End of Time, page 315.—Device—a rose crossing a scythe; within the angle of the scythe, an hour-glass.

Mother and Child, page 318.—Mr. William Sharp published, in *The Atlantic Monthly* for June 1895, a very sympathetic and interesting article, *Some Reminiscences of Christina Rossetti*. Here he says that on one occasion Dante Gabriel "pointed out that Blake might have written the four verses called *Mother and Child*." It would seem truer to say that Blake might have written a lyric, of higher quality, embodying much the same conception. Device — some flowers of undefined genus, with sun-rays behind them.

On the Death of a Cat, page 319. — This cat belonged to our aunt, Eliza Harriet Polidori. Device — a cat, in a rather sentimental attitude of languor, extending its right arm over a kitten. The cat is sandy and white, the kitten tabby.

Love Defended, page 322. — Device — a blind man (stanza 3) groping, with trees in the background.

The Martyr, page 323. — Device — the soul of the martyr received into heaven by an angel. Between the angel's wings are a series of red and white curves, symbolizing (I suppose) the seven heavens, as in Dante.

The Dying Man to his Betrothed, page 325. — Device — a rosebush intertwined by a snake.

The Time of Waiting, page 334. — Device — a damsel on a steep green slope, stretching her arms up longingly; from the sky a black-hooded woman, or spectre, addresses her with an action of admonition. This seems to be apposite chiefly to triplet 2.

Tasso and Leonora, page 337. — Device — the shooting star in a female form.

Resurrection Eve, page 341. — Device — a white grave-cross, two palm shrubs interlacing above it; in the sky, crescent moon and star.

The Dream, page 356. — I am not sure whether the first short quatrain here printed is an integral portion of the poem, or rather a quotation from some other writer; I fancy the latter.

Eleanor, page 358. — This may be a portrait from the life — I know not now of whom.

Isidora, page 359. — Maturin's romance *Melmoth the Wanderer* is, I suppose, still known to several readers: it was republished some few years ago. Yet it may be as well to say, in explanation of the present poem, that Melmoth is a personage who has made a compact with the Devil, thereby securing an enormous length of life (say a century and a half), and the power of flitting at will from land to land. At the end of the term, Melmoth's soul is to be forfeited, unless he can meanwhile induce some one else to take the compact off his hands.

Melmoth makes numerous efforts in this direction, but all abortive. One of his intended victims is a beautiful girl named Immalee, a child of Nature in an Indian island — a second Miranda. She becomes deeply enamoured of Melmoth, but resists his tamperings with her soul. She is finally identified as the daughter of a Spanish Grandee, and is then baptized as Isidora. At one point of the story she espouses Melmoth, and bears him a child. Christina's poem is her deathbed scene. The last line is truly a fine stroke of pathos and of effect; but it is not Christina's — it comes *verbatim* out of Maturin.

Zara, page 362. — See the note on the poem *Look on this picture, and on this* (p. 103). In the novel of *Women*, Zara is the rival (she finally turns out to be the mother) of Eva; she is a shining leader of society, much the same sort of character as Lady Montrevor in *The Wild Irish Boy* (p. 14). In the same year, 1847, when she wrote *Zara*, my sister wrote a separate composition, *Eva*. Its merit is but middling, and I do not reproduce it here. The device to *Zara* is a foxglove plant, with insects sucking its poison-honey.

Immalee, page 366. — See the note on *Isidora* (p. 359).

Lady Isabella, page 366. — This was Lady Isabella Howard, a daughter of the Earl of Wicklow; she was a pupil of my aunt, Charlotte Polidori. My sister entertained an ardent admiration for the loveliness of character and person which marked this young lady, who died of a decline at the age of eighteen or thereabouts.

Night and Death, page 367. — It may reasonably be assumed that this lyric also has some reference to the death of Lady Isabella Howard.

The Lotus-Eaters, page 370. — Of course the sentiment here, as well as the title, comes to some considerable extent out of Tennyson.

THE END

WORKS BY WILLIAM WATSON.

THE POEMS OF WILLIAM WATSON.

A New Edition Rearranged by the Author, with Additions and a New Frontispiece Portrait.

12mo. Cloth, gilt top. $1.25.

"Is full of the rich charm of genius, and we admire him for the English patriotism that thrills through his English song." — *The Independent.*

"His name will fill a proud place among the poets of his day, for his fame will increase with the years, as his poetry is of the sort that stands the test of time." — *The World.*

"Lovers of poise, felicity, and beauty, will find this volume worth its weight in gold. It stirs one anew to those ecstasies of emotion without which this life, however well regulated by reason, becomes a dull round of arid pleasures and vexatious pains." — *Boston Traveler.*

LYRIC LOVE.

An Anthology.

Golden Treasury Series. 16mo. $1.00.

"This anthology represents the choicest flowers of English love poetry gathered from three centuries of song. The editor was fastidious, and his aim was far from merely collecting love lyrics, for it includes the bringing together, whenever practicable, of the best English poetry having love as its personal inspiration and objective theme. Thus, many passages, where the primal agency was love, have been selected from plays and from narrative verse, when they could be detached from the context without impairing their integrity. The range of selection is wide, and the anthology is guided by the best of taste. 'Lyric Love' forms a good second to the peerless 'Golden Treasury' of Professor Palgrave, and it has the advantage of including some beautiful specimens of modern love, and many old songs which have no place in other collections." — *Philadelphia Public Ledger.*

THE ELOPING ANGELS.

A Caprice.

Cloth. Small Square 8vo. 75 cents.

"It is well executed, and marked with the author's usual lucidity and beauty of expression." — *Boston Transcript.*

"The plan and development of this metrical story are novel, and the versification is marked by the finish and smoothness which distinguishes all of the poet's productions. He is always happy in his choice of phrases to express succinctly his meaning; and though the treatment of his subject is in the main light and humorous, the work has a more serious purpose that cannot be misunderstood." — *Boston Saturday Evening Gazette.*

MACMILLAN & CO.,

66 FIFTH AVENUE, NEW YORK.

The Humours of the Court:
A COMEDY.
AND OTHER POEMS.

BY

ROBERT BRIDGES.

12mo.   Gilt top.   Price $1.25.

SELECTIONS
FROM THE
Poems of Aubrey de Vere.
EDITED WITH A PREFACE

BY

GEORGE EDWARD WOODBERRY.

WITH PORTRAIT.

12mo.   Cloth. $1.25.

"This is a most interesting collection of poems. It is of great historical worth and should be in every home." — *New Haven Leader.*

"Poetry that is noble, dignified, and imaginative." — *Hartford Courant.*

"The style is virile and chaste, and the thoughts are often lofty; the legends of old Ireland are given with poetic power and patriotic spirit." — *Public Opinion.*

MACMILLAN & CO.,
66 FIFTH AVENUE, NEW YORK.